John Augustine Zahm

Catholic Science and Catholic Scientists

John Augustine Zahm
Catholic Science and Catholic Scientists
ISBN/EAN: 9783337419677

Printed in Europe, USA, Canada, Australia, Japan

Cover: Foto ©Lupo / pixelio.de

More available books at **www.hansebooks.com**

CATHOLIC SCIENCE

AND

CATHOLIC SCIENTISTS.

BY

THE REV. J. A. ZAHM, C.S.C.,

PROFESSOR OF PHYSICS IN THE UNIVERSITY OF NOTRE DAME.

The source of science is the fount of truth.
    The vibrant waves of heat, of quivering light,
    The ebb and flow of time from day to night,
Are pulses from a heart of endless youth.

We gaze in wonder as the stream grows wide,
    And cry, "Behold this boundless power!"
    Forgetful that it is Religion's dower
To guide the waters as the moon the tide.

PHILADELPHIA:
H. L. KILNER & CO.
1893.

TO

MY BROTHER,

ALBERT F. ZAHM, A. M., M. E.,

THIS BOOK

IS AFFECTIONATELY DEDICATED.

PREFACE.

This volume is composed of articles, revised and augmented, which originally appeared, the first two in the *Ave Maria*, the last two in the *American Catholic Quarterly Review*. They are republished in book form in response to numerous requests from patrons of the Catholic Summer School, from members of various Reading Circles, and from distinguished representatives of the hierarchy. The object of the book, as will appear from its perusal, is to exhibit in a brief compass the relation of the Church to science, and to show that, in the words of Cardinal Newman, "Religious truth is not only a portion but a condition of knowledge;" that there is not, and cannot be, a conflict between real science and true religion; that those who have been guided by the light of faith and Christian philosophy are precisely those who have achieved the greatest measure of success in the pursuit of knowledge, and have contributed most toward securing those glorious results, in every department of science, of which the modern intellectual world is so justly proud.

J. A. ZAHM, C. S. C.

NOTRE DAME, IND., May 22, 1893.

CONTENTS.

CHAPTER I.
SCIENCE AND THE CHURCH 9

CHAPTER II.
CATHOLIC SCIENTISTS AND THEIR ACHIEVEMENTS . 55

CHAPTER III.
CATHOLIC DOGMA AND SCIENTIFIC DOGMATISM . . 118

CHAPTER IV.
THE FRIENDS AND THE FOES OF SCIENCE 163

CATHOLIC SCIENCE
AND
CATHOLIC SCIENTISTS.

CHAPTER I.

SCIENCE AND THE CHURCH.

AMONG the many questions that have engaged the attention of thinking minds, especially within the last few years, none has excited a livelier or a more widespread interest than that concerning the relation between religion and science, or, more especially, the relation between modern science and the Catholic Church. Among those who let others do their thinking for them, or who are content to get their information second-hand (as it is too often, alas! doled out to them in garbled articles by an infidel press), and even among those whose intellectual acquirements should teach them better, there seems to be an impression—and, in many instances, a conviction—that there is a conflict between the teachings of the Church and the truths of science; that the doctrines of the former can no longer be reconciled with the conclusions of the latter; that, in a word, if the Church wishes to keep abreast with the advance of science, she will not only have to modify many of her dogmas, but will be forced to abandon some of them entirely as no longer tenable. Then, again, this impression, or conviction, of these good people is confirmed by what they have heard or read about the attitude of the Church toward science in ages gone by. They have been told that the Church is the enemy of progress; that she not only does not now, but never did, encourage scientific research; and they are ever ready to point to instances which they consider as verifying such views. They adduce as facts of sober history tales of libraries burned, genius hampered and persecuted, and finish the charge with some terrible episode in the lives of the "Martyrs of Science."

It is some of these points that we wish to discuss in the present article. We shall consider some of the objections brought forward by modern science against the teachings of the Church, and then define as clearly and succinctly as may be the nature and scope of science and religion, and state what now is, what always has been, and what ever must be the relation between human science and the Church of God.

But although we have it in purpose to speak of the Church in her relation to modern science, it is by no means our intention to come forward as the Church's apologist.

The Church needs no apologists. Her past history is her apology. Her *raison d'être* is seen in the miraculous transformation she has effected in the moral, social, and intellectual condition of mankind since her advent into this world. All the civilization and enlightenment we now enjoy, all that is great and good and noble in the world, all that is pure, grand, and sublime in humanity, is due to her. It was she that made the present condition of the world possible; it is she that we have to thank for all the advantages and blessings, in the natural as well as in the spiritual order, that are now ours. Without her progress and civilization, as we now understand them, would have been impossible; without her we should to-day be no better than was the world when the Church entered upon her mission of refining and spiritualizing nearly nineteen centuries ago.

Neither is it our intention in any statements we may make to minimize, even in the slightest degree, any doctrine the Church proposes for our belief, or assert anything that is inconsistent with the strictest orthodoxy, or, if you will, with the most pronounced Ultramontanism.

The Church has no retractions to make; she knows not what it is to make concessions in what she has once defined to be of faith. How, then, can one who pretends to be a Catholic do what the Church has never done and never can do? Conscious of her divine origin, of the Spirit of Truth being always with her to assist her and preserve her from error, she continues her office of teacher of the nations, despite all that the world may say or do against her.

Such, then, being the spirit of the Church, there is only one course open for those who would be her children, and that is to follow faithfully the path she has marked out for them. No liberalism, then, in matters of doctrine can be tolerated; no concessions can be allowed. What the Church teaches *must* be accepted as divine truth—all that so-called science may teach to the contrary notwithstanding.

With these few premises, we shall at once proceed to examine some of the difficulties that modern science is thought to have raised against the teachings of Revelation. The objections generally brought forward, and those to which most interest attaches, are those which have been rendered plausible by recent studies in geology, biology, and astronomy. There are others, it is true, that have been suggested by investigations and discoveries in other departments of science; but the arguments drawn from the sciences just mentioned are those on which the Rationalist most relies in his controversies with the defenders of revealed truth.

The principal objections made by geologists

against the Bible are based on certain passages of the book of Genesis, and notably on interpretations that have been given to the first chapter. The objections are as far-reaching as they are interesting; and, if they were well founded, we might indeed despair of ever seeing a reconciliation between the teachings of science on the one hand and those of religion on the other. They embrace, among others, such questions as the age of the world, the six days of creation, the origin and antiquity of man, the unity of species, and the nature and extent of the Noachian deluge. Now, although there is material in each of these subjects for one or even many articles, we think it possible to give them all a satisfactory notice in this paper, and that, too, without making any unreasonable demand on either the time or the patience of our readers.

And, first, as to the age of the world. Astronomers and geologists tell us that millions—yea, hundreds of millions—of years must have elapsed since the creation of the world—if, indeed, the world be not eternal—and hence, they say, science is in direct contradiction to the generally received opinion which places the age of the world at about six thousand years.

But here, at the outset, our learned astronomers and geologists make several serious blunders. They mistake a generally received opinion for a doctrine or definition of the Church; whereas, as a matter of fact, the Church has never defined anything regarding the age of the world, and most probably never will, as the age of the world has nothing whatever to do—at least as far as we can see—with the object of her teaching, viz. faith and morals.

Again, we are told that the conclusions of science respecting the age of the world are at variance with Scripture, when, in reality, the Bible nowhere says anything whatever about the matter, so far as the age of the world is concerned, except what is contained in the first words of Genesis: *In principio creavit Deus cœlum et terram*—" In the *beginning* God created heaven and earth." But when was the beginning? No one knows. Nothing can be more indefinite. It may have been six thousand years ago, as some have thought; or it may have been, as Proctor and others contend, five hundred million years ago. Scripture says nothing on the subject more definite than the words quoted, and the Church has never made any declaration whatever; so that scientists are given all the latitude they could desire, as far as time is concerned. True it is, there have been commentators on the Sacred Text who, thinking that the creation of the world was simultaneous with the creation of man—and it must be pleaded in their behalf that when they wrote there was no special reason for believing that the case was otherwise—have maintained that the age of the world is about six thousand years; but then the opinions of commentators, however learned, are by no means to be confounded with authoritative teachings of the Church. As well might we say that the theories and hypotheses of individual scientists are always to be accepted as demonstrated truths, as facts that cannot be gainsaid. If this distinction between opinion and doctrine, between theory and demonstration, were always borne in mind, we should hear less of the alleged conflict between science and religion. What the conflict should be called—what, in fact, it always has been—is a conflict between individuals; commentators and theologians on one side, and scientists and philosophers on the other.

The second objection urged regards the days of creation. It was long considered—and, indeed, there was no particular reason for holding a different opinion until lately, when the study of geology began to open new avenues of thought—that the six days spoken of in Genesis were the ordinary days of twenty-four hours each. But geology and astronomy come forward and tell us that their records speak of untold æons that must have elapsed during those six days, and consequently that the Bible is again at fault. The Sacred Text is once more examined, and it is found that the days spoken of do not necessarily mean periods of twenty-four hours each, but that they may be interpreted as meaning indefinite periods of time.

Nay, more: there is strong presumptive evidence for believing even from Scripture that the days referred to were not true solar days, but that, on the contrary, they were periods of time, just such as geologists and astronomers demand. According to Scripture, the sun was not created until the fourth day; consequently, there was no alternation of day and night as we now know it, and no way of dividing time into days of twenty-four hours each, like that which existed after the sun appeared on the fourth day.

But this interpretation is not a new one, or one that has been provoked by the advance of modern science. True, recent scientific investigations have caused this interpretation to be the one now generally accepted; but as far back as the time of St. Augustine, and even further, the difficulty of considering the days of Genesis as ordinary solar days was apparent. Indeed, the saint himself, in his masterly work on Genesis, inclines to the opinion, as being more reasonable, that the days spoken of were indefinite periods of time. In this opinion he is followed by the greatest theologians and commentators of the Middle Ages—among others, Albertus Magnus and the angel of the schools, St. Thomas Aquinas.

The angelic doctor says that the opinion according to which the days of Genesis are solar days is plainer and the one more conformable to the letter of the text; but, as if foreseeing the discussions the biblical narrative would eventually give rise to, declares the opinion which makes the days periods of time to be the more reasonable, and the better adapted to defend the sacred Scriptures from the ridicule of unbelievers, and adds that it is the one that pleases him most. And this opinion—it can never, we think, be considered as more than an opinion, not originated by modern science, although given new weight and rendered more probable by recent discoveries,—this opinion, maintained by St. Augustine and the great doctors of the Church during the Middle Ages, is the one now almost universally accepted. As in the case of the age of the world, the Church has never pronounced upon the subject, and most likely never will. It is an opinion that does not in the slightest degree militate against any of her teachings; and, far from being contrary to any of the declarations of Scripture, is the only one which, even aside from the light thrown on the subject by science, seems tenable. It is consequently an opinion that any one is free to choose and defend. As a Catholic, then, one is at perfect liberty, so far as the dogmas of the Church are concerned, to consider the days of Genesis as true solar days or as indefinite periods of time.

But it may be urged that there are more serious objections to be answered before science and Scripture can be harmonized. What about the difficulties concerning the origin and antiquity of man, and about the unity of the human species, put forward by a class of scientists who call themselves evolutionists? What, in a word, about evolution?

It is scarcely necessary to state that it would be simply impossible, in a brief article like this, to give anything like a detailed answer to this question, or even to give a *resumé* of what evolutionists actually teach. The subject of evolution, although but little discussed until about a third of a century ago (the time of the appearance of Darwin's work on the *Origin of Species*), is now one that excites more interest than any other one subject whatever. It already has a literature of its own, and the number of works pertaining to the question is daily increasing. It is treated of in magazines and newspapers; it is discussed from the rostrum and the pulpit; and it is a frequent topic of conversation in the railway-car and in the drawing-room. Everybody talks about evolution, and often, too, without knowing any more about the matter than the fact that some one who is an evolutionist says that man is descended from a monkey. Still, although we cannot give even a *resumé* of the teachings of evolutionists, we can state a few facts and principles—sufficient, however, to answer our present purpose.

One of the fundamental teachings of evolution, and the one about which we are just now most particularly concerned, is that which declares that all the higher forms of life, animal and vegetable, have been derived, by the interaction of natural causes, from the lower forms, and that the lowest and first forms of organic life were produced by the action of the forces of nature on inorganic matter. On this one point all evolutionists agree, although there is a great variety of opinions as to the causes that have operated and the processes that have obtained in the gradual development of the organic world from its first beginnings to what it is now. For what we shall have to say on the subject, however, this difference of opinion is of no moment.

Now, at the outset we must premise that evolution is at its best only a theory, only an hypothesis. It is simply an assumption—and an assumption, too, that rests on other assumptions. No one who has studied the question with even moderate care, and who understands the distinction between theory and doctrine, between hypothesis and demonstrated fact, will pretend to say it is anything more. It assumes, in the first place, the truth of Laplace's mechanical explanation of the formation of the universe as put forth in his celebrated nebular hypothesis—an hypothesis which maintained that the earth and all the heavenly bodies once existed in a state of incandescent vapor; were once immense clouds of fire-mist,*

---

* The view that the primitive nebulous matter of the universe was in an incandescent condition is now being abandoned by scientists.

which, after the lapse of countless ages, were condensed into the solid orbs we now behold. From the very nature of the case this is an hypothesis whose truth can never be demonstrated. It may be shown by astronomers, physicists, and geologists to be more or less plausible, but it can never get above the rank of a theory. It is, if we will, the best mechanical explanation of the formation of the universe that has yet been given; but it is nothing more than an attempt to account for what can never be known with any certainty without a special divine revelation—a revelation which one can safely assert will never be made.

Again, evolution assumes that organic was derived from inorganic matter by the simple interaction of the forces of nature.

In the words of Prof. Huxley: "If the hypothesis of evolution be true, living matter must have arisen from non-living matter; for by the hypothesis the condition of the globe was at one time such that living matter could not have existed on it—life being entirely incompatible with the gaseous state." It assumes the truth of the theory of spontaneous generation, and that, too, in the face of unanswerable—we might say conclusive—scientific evidence against it. Any one who has followed the investigations on the subject by the eminent French *savant* M. Pasteur, or watched the delicate and ingenious experiments devised by Prof. Tyndall, will, we think, be forced to admit, whatever may have been his preconceived notions, the force of their arguments, and to acknowledge the justness of their conclusions against the possibility of spontaneous generation. Since the researches of these eminent experimentalists were made known, no one laying any claim to scientific knowledge has thought of regarding spontaneous generation as anything more than an old and exploded theory. Even Darwin himself considered spontaneous generation as "a result absolutely inconceivable." Dr. Carpenter, one of the most eminent biologists of the age, regarded it as an "astounding hypothesis;" whilst the celebrated Dr. Virchow, at the conference of the German naturalists and physicians at Munich in 1877, did not hesitate to declare that it was a "theory not supported by any evidence," and as one "utterly discredited."

Then, again, as a third postulate, evolution assumes as a fact the transmutation of species, the change suddenly or gradually of one species, of either animal or plant, into another. But this is an assumption for which there is not the slightest evidence whatever. Not a single fact in the whole range of natural science can be adduced favoring the truth of the transmutation of species; not a single instance can be cited of a single species, whether of plant or animal, that has ever, either through the agency of natural causes or by the artifice of man, been changed into another species.

The bird-fancier and the florist can produce varieties, but species never. There have been produced by cultivation different varieties of roses, different varieties of pigeons, but there is not on record a solitary example of the change of one species of pigeon or of one species of rose into another species.

And yet, if there were any truth in the theory of the transmutation of species, some conclusive evidence in support of it should certainly have been discovered before this. For hundreds of years there have been thousands of observers of thousands of species and of millions of individuals of animals and plants in all parts of the world, and yet not a single fact has been brought to light to justify a theory that is absolutely essential to the hypothesis of evolution. According to the calculation of probabilities, the present chances against the transmutation of species, and consequently against evolution, are as infinity to nothing. Even Prof. Huxley, with all his evolutionary tendencies, is forced to admit, in speaking of the Darwinian hypothesis, that "it is our clear conviction that, as the evidence stands, it is not absolutely proven that a group of animals having all the characters exhibited by species in nature has ever been originated by selection, whether artificial or natural."

If, then, there is no evidence for the transmutation of one species into another in the lower forms of life, we find still less when we come to consider the change of one of the higher animal forms into man. Between the brute creation and man there is an impassable chasm. Between the most perfectly developed ape and man, with all his wonderful gifts of mind and soul, there is an infinite distance that no " missing link," and no series of missing links, can bridge over. From the highest exhibition of brute instinct to the lowest manifestation of human reason there is a void as great as that which separates earth from heaven.

Such are a few of the assumptions of the evolutionist, every one of which is absolutely necessary to the establishment of the truth of his hypothesis, and yet none of them has any demonstrated foundation in fact. What, then, is our conclusion as regards evolution and faith? Evidently, to say the least, that evolution has proven nothing against the teachings of faith, from the simple fact that evolution, so far, is at best a conjecture, a theory, not only unproven, but a theory that, as it is now taught, would seem to be unprovable.

But supposing the nebular hypothesis and spontaneous generation and the transmutation of species, and all the other postulates necessary to establish the fact of evolution, be granted; supposing that, as new facts are discovered, and as nature is more carefully scrutinized, it be shown that there has obtained that development from lower to higher forms of life that the evolutionist speaks of,—what then? We might reply that it would be time enough to answer the question when the evidence is forthcoming; but, as it seems to bear somewhat closely on the subject we are discussing, and as, even aside from this, its answer, if not altogether new, may have a certain interest for some of our readers—at least, as illustrative of the liberty of thought that the Catholic enjoys regarding this and similar questions—we deem it best to give it a passing notice.

Before going further, however, it will be necessary to state more precisely the meaning of a few terms. We have given a general definition of evolution, yet one that will answer our purpose sufficiently well. But as all who hold the doctrine are not at one as to the causes and processes that have obtained, it will be well to define the beliefs of the principal classes of evolutionists. First, then, we have the atheistic evolutionist, or the evolutionist who denies the existence of a divine Creator. To this class belong Hæckel, Vogt, and Büchner, and many of their disciples in Europe and in this country. The second class comprises the school of agnostic evolutionists—those, namely, who, while not professing faith in the existence of a divine Creator, still do not explicitly deny His existence. They simply relegate God to the Unknowable, because, they say, we can know nothing about Him. Among the more prominent representatives of this school are Herbert

Spencer, Tyndall, Huxley, and Bain. Evolutionists of the third class are theists, or those who profess and maintain a belief in the existence of a personal God. To this last class belong the ablest scientists and philosophers of the age. Among those best known we may mention the names of Owen, Sir John Herschel, Sir William Thompson, Prof. A. Gray, Mr. Wallace, M. Naudin, M. Albert Gaudry, Mivart, Quatrefages, and scores of others.

It is quite evident that a Catholic could not hold the theory of evolution in the sense in which it is maintained by atheists and agnostics. To do so would be in direct opposition to the first article of his creed. But could he, consistently with his faith, hold it as taught by theists? Before answering this question we must properly understand another term of paramount importance in the discussion of the subject. That term is creation. Creation, in its primary and strictest sense, is the origination by God of something without pre-existing material. But, besides this primary or absolute creation, there is also a secondary or derivative creation, which obtains, for instance, when God, after having created matter directly, gives to it the power of evolving under certain conditions into all the various forms it may subsequently assume. In the first instance, God creates matter absolutely; and then, by giving it certain powers and properties—in other words, by imposing on it what we call natural laws—creates potentially all the forms that may afterward be evolved from matter thus under the action of the forces and properties given it.

Now the question comes again, Is there anything in the theistic idea of evolution contrary to the declaration of Scripture or to the teachings of Catholic faith? We are not proclaiming a novelty or giving expression to a heterodox opinion when we state it as our belief that there is not. According to the words of Genesis, God did not create animals and plants in the primary sense of the word, but caused them to be produced from preexisting material. "Let the earth bring forth," "Let the waters bring forth," He says, showing clearly that creation in these instances was only secondary or derivative.

So far, then, the way seems clear. But was this creation instantaneous, or was it something effected only after the lapse of time through the operation of natural forces; were the animals and plants called immediately into existence from crude inorganic material by the *fiat* of Omnipotence, or were they slowly and gradually evolved from this same inorganic material, and developed from lower to higher forms in accordance with laws that God Himself had established in the beginning?

It is popularly supposed that the creations spoken of were instantaneous; but the evolutionist—we mean the theistic evolutionist—contends that they were gradual, and the result of the interaction, according to divinely preordained laws, of natural forces on matter. In either case the creative act of God is conserved; and in the second case, it seems to us, as much as in the first. The evolutionist simply maintains that God did potentially what the ordinary scriptural interpreter believes He did by a distinct exercise of infinite power.

Thus understood, then, it seems clear that there is nothing in evolution contrary to Scripture. But may there not be some dogmatic definition of the Church against it, or may it not be contrary, at least in its spirit, to the teachings of the Fathers and Doctors of the Church?

As to the Church, she has never pronounced on the matter, and there is not—we speak under correction—a single definition that declares, even by implication, that evolution is opposed to faith. But we must go still further. We are not satisfied by steering clear of opinions that are manifestly heretical; we wish also to avoid, much less advocate, opinions that a *consensus* of theological authority would consider as rash or dangerous. What, then, do the Doctors and Fathers of the Church say in relation to the subject? It need not be observed that they could not have said anything about evolution as we now understand it, for the simple reason that the subject, as taught to-day, was to them quite unknown. But, still, they may have laid down principles that will meet all our difficulties. And that they did so is a fact, we think, no one who weighs what they have written can deny.

In his great work on Genesis, St. Augustine, when speaking of the creation of animals and plants, repeats time and again his belief that they were brought into existence by the operation of natural causes. He tells us explicitly that they were created potentially, and that they were afterward developed into the manifold forms we now behold. "As," he teaches, "the seed contains invisibly within itself all that is found in the full-grown tree, so also the world, after its creation by God, contained all the germs of the various forms of life that were afterward produced."

St. Thomas follows St. Augustine's teaching regarding derivative creation, as do also the great Jesuit theologian Saurez and many others of acknowledged authority. We shall not trench on the time of our readers in making quotations or references, as it is not our purpose to give a treatise on the subject, but only to point out a few well-authenticated facts. Those who have the leisure or the inclination can make a detailed examination of the question for themselves.

Thus, then, we see that the system of evolution which acknowledges God as direct Creator of matter and force, and as at least the indirect Creator—a Creator through secondary causes—

of all the manifold forms of organic nature that we know of, is not inconsistent with either the declarations of Scripture, the definitions of the Church, or the teachings of the Doctors and Fathers. Consequently, as matters now stand, evolution is not contrary to Catholic faith, and any one is at liberty to hold the theory if he is satisfied with the evidence adduced in its support.

But, it may be asked, can this system of evolution be made, consistently with Catholic doctrine, to embrace also man? In answer to this question we shall simply observe that, as to the soul of man, the reply must be a decided negative. Each individual soul, according to Catholic teaching, is created directly and absolutely by God Himself. But as to whether theistic evolution may embrace man's body, considered as separate from and independent of the soul, it may be remarked that the theory has been defended among others by no less an authority than the eminent Catholic naturalist and philosopher St. George Mivart: and we are not aware that his position has been proven by theologians to be untenable. The hypothesis may be rash, and even dangerous, but we do not think that, considering it simply in its bearing on dogma, any one could pronounce it as certainly and positively false. But—and this is important to bear in mind —it is at most a matter of mere speculation, and such it will probably always remain.

So also is the evolution of the lower forms of

animal and plant life only a theory—"a fascinating theory," as the great Agassiz called it—but nothing more. Organic forms *may* have been evolved according to the laws of theistic evolution, but *were* they? We are now dealing with a question of fact, not of fancy. To this we may reply, with the eminent German physiologist Du Bois-Reymond, when facing a similar question, "*Ignoramus et ignorabimus*—we do not know, and we never shall know." We know that God has created all things that exist. How He has created them is a mystery that does not concern us. We know that all that is grand and sublime and beautiful in nature is the work of His hands, although we may never know anything more than we do now of the wonderful methods and processes employed. Probably we should show more wisdom by humbly acknowledging that we are dealing with one of those mysteries of the natural order of which a solution will never be vouchsafed us in this world. At any rate, whatever advances science may make, we can rest secure in the thought that there is nothing in evolution, outside of the atheistic and agnostic systems of it, that contravenes the teachings of Holy Church. For us this is sufficient.

Having thus disposed of that insurmountable barrier, as unbelievers are pleased to call it, which evolution is ordinarily considered to oppose to a consistent acceptance of revealed truth, we shall now proceed to those other subjects that are at the present time regarded as offering special difficulties to the theologian. We refer to the much-vexed questions of the unity of species, the antiquity of man, and the Noachian deluge.

The question of the unity of the human species is one that, more or less, has engaged the attention of philosophers for centuries. But the impetus given to the study of biological science, particularly within the last thirty years, has created for the subject an interest it never possessed before. It has been taken up not only by speculative scientists and sentimental philanthropists, but also, and especially, by practical, learned, truth-loving naturalists, philologists, ethnologists, and archæologists the world over. All the races and tribes of the earth have been visited in the interests of science; their anatomical and physiological characteristics have been noted and compared; their manners and customs have been studied with scrupulous care; their languages and literatures have been consulted by scholars of every shade of opinion; their monuments and records have been ransacked to satisfy the demands of *savants* and learned societies; their traditions and religious beliefs have been examined even in their minutest details. The hieroglyphical writings of the ancient Egyptians have been deciphered; the cuneiform inscriptions of Western Asia interpreted; the remains of prehistoric man in the Old and New Worlds questioned; and all this with what result? One in perfect harmony with the teachings of the Church, which maintains, and ever has maintained, the oneness of the human species.

The bearing of her doctrine of the unity of species—*i. e.* that all mankind is derived from common parents—on some of the fundamental teachings of faith is so evident as to need no comment. But precise as the doctrine of the Church is on this point, its truth has not been in the least impaired by the investigations and discoveries of modern science. On the contrary, all demonstrated conclusions in every department of knowledge have, as every Catholic knew would be the case, only tended to corroborate what the Church has always taught, and to strengthen more than ever her position in the eyes of the intellectual world. We know that there have been men with theories to support—specialists who wished to obtain notoriety—who have maintained the unprovable hypothesis of the multiplicity of species. We are aware also that there have been those who have divided mankind into species according to geographical distribution or color or language; but no one has ever regarded their theories as anything more than vague and unfounded conjectures.

Another and more interesting question is that regarding the antiquity of man. Scientific men now maintain that man has been on earth much longer than is popularly supposed, and much longer, too, than is consistent with the declarations of the Sacred Text. Instead of the six thousand years that are generally assigned as the time that has elapsed since man appeared on the earth, scientists assure us that his advent dates back much farther. Some will tell us that man has inhabited this earth for at least 40,000 or 50,000 years; whilst others, like Sir John Lubbock and Charles Lyell, will claim for him an antiquity of 200,000 years, and still others more than a million. They tell us that the remains of prehistoric man, the instruments of defence and the chase, found in Europe and America, teach us that all our ideas about his antiquity have to be entirely modified.

Now, at the first blush, the great disagreement among the scientists themselves about the question at issue should put us on our guard. No two of them view the question in the same light. No two of them, in any given instance, ever arrive at the same conclusion as the result of their investigations. Geologists particularly are fond of giving a great antiquity to man, and to the period during which animal and vegetable life has existed upon this earth. According to Lyell, the life-period of the earth must be somewhere about 300,000,000 years. Yet, in the face of this statement, the great mathematicians and physicists Sir Wm. Thompson and Prof. Tait come forward, with conclusions based on well-known laws of physics, and assert as a certainty that it would have been simply impossible for life, as we now know it, to have existed on the earth for more than 10,000,000 or 15,000,000 years at most—only the one-thirtieth or the one-twentieth of the time claimed by Lyell and his followers. Prof. Tait's own words, as found in his admirable work, *Recent Advances in Physical Science*, are: "We can at once say to geologists that, granting this premise, that physical laws have remained as they are now, and that we know of all the physical laws which have been operating during that time, we cannot give more time for their speculation than about ten, or, say, at most, fifteen, million years. But we dare say many of you are acquainted with the speculations of Lyell and others, especially of Darwin, who tells us that even for a comparatively brief portion of geological history three hundred millions of years will not suffice. We say, so much the worse for geology as at present understood by its chief authorities, for, as you will presently see, physical considerations, from various independent points of view, render it utterly impossible that more than ten million years can be granted."

Now, looking at Lyell's proportion of man's age to that of the life-period of the earth—viz. 200,000 to 300,000,000; *i.e.* 1 to 1500—in the light of Thompson's conclusions, we find that the age of man must, according to Lyell's own figures, be brought down to a period somewhere between 6600 and 10,000 years. The mean result, which, however, is only approximate, would be about 8000 years. Still, it is equally decisive as against the unwarranted assumptions of geologists.

But what about the antiquity of man according to the Bible? It is a mistaken idea to suppose that the Scriptures give any date as to the creation of man, or any definite data that would aid one in calculating how long he has been upon the earth. The dates usually put at the head of chapters or parts of the Bible are not a part of the inspired writings, but only the determinations of individual commentators from such data as the Sacred Text afforded them. These data, often vague and uncertain, are mostly the genealogies of the patriarchs, reigns of kings, periods of servitude, etc., and, owing to various causes, which it is unnecessary to explain at present, it is found that even the oldest texts of the Bible we now possess—viz. the Septuagint, the Hebrew, and the Samaritan—seriously differ from one another in their chronologies.

No orthodox writer, according to Riccioli, an eminent Jesuit astronomer, places the era of creation of man higher than 7000 B. C. or lower than 3700. Of two hundred different values collected by the chronologer Des Vignolles, who wrote more than a century and a half ago, for the time elapsed from the creation of man until the coming of Christ, the least was 3483 and the greatest 6984 years, giving a difference of 3501 years. Adding to these results the time that has elapsed since the coming of Christ (1893 years), we have as a minimum of man's antiquity 5376 years, and as a maximum 8877 years. The mean of these two sums would be a little over 7000 years—a result that chronologists hold to be better founded than the popularly received figure that places the age of our race at about 6000 years. In conclusion, we would observe that it is now considered, by those who have made biblical chronology a study, that, from the data given in the Bible, it is probable that the time which has elapsed since the creation of our first parents has been about 8000 or 10,000 years. It may have been a little more; but, judging from the data calculated from, it is probably a little less.

Here, then, we have, on the one hand, the latest conclusions—the results are only approximate—of science, which put the antiquity of man at about 8000 or 10,000 years; and, on the other hand, the computations of biblical chronologists, which, giving a latitude of fully thirty-five centuries between the lowest and the highest values, afford certainly all the time that the geologist or astronomer can prove necessary to reconcile the facts of his science with the known data of Holy Scripture.

So far as the Church is concerned, the antiquity of man is an open question. She has never pronounced on the subject, but, as in many similar instances, has left it to be decided by learned men according to the data afforded by chronological investigations.

In the calculations to which we have just alluded we have taken the results of geologists whose views on the subject are extreme. But there are not wanting eminent scholars in every branch of modern scientific inquiry who maintain that the antiquity of man is far less than some of our "advanced thinkers" would make it, and that there is yet no valid reason for considering it greater than it has been popularly supposed to be—viz. 6000 years. At all events—barring all fanciful computations, like those based on Indian or Chinese chronologies; or idle conjectures, like those founded on the relics discovered in Scandinavian graves, in French peat- or gravel-beds, or in Swiss lake-dwellings—there is certainly no conflict between science—we do not mean *theory*—and religion on the subject of the age of our race. More than this: as fully convinced as we are that there is no conflict now, so fully are we persuaded that there never will be any; but that, on the contrary, every new scientific discovery, when properly understood, will, as in every other case, only tend to confirm the teachings of the inspired record.

One more difficulty, and we have done with the objections we proposed to answer. We are told that there is a conflict between the teachings of science and the account of the Flood as contained in the Bible. We might admit that there is a conflict between the teachings of certain scientists and the Bible, but this would prove nothing against the Bible. That there is even the slightest conflict between the Mosaic narrative of the Deluge and the demonstrated conclusions of science we emphatically deny.

It is the popular belief—a belief, too, that the words of the Bible seem to favor—that the Flood was universal; but science steps forward and tells us that, for many reasons we need not mention, the Deluge could not have been universal. Admitting, as we may, that there was nothing more miraculous about the Deluge than the employment by God, at a fixed time, of physical agents, as we now know them, for the accomplishment of His purpose—the destruction of the human race in punishment of their crimes—we do not see that we are obliged, even by the words of Scripture, to believe that the Deluge was universal as to the surface of the earth, but universal only, with the exception of those in the ark, as to man. The end for which the Flood was sent—the washing away of the wicked from the face of the earth—would have been attained as well by a local as by a general deluge. The frequent use of universal for particular terms in every part of the Sacred Text is well known. But there is no reason whatever why the terms employed in the narrative of the Flood should be used in a general rather than a particular sense; and the Church, as in the other cases we have spoken of, has not given any decision on the question. Hence, in the present state of the discussion, we are at perfect liberty to believe that the waters covered the whole earth, or extended over only that portion—a very limited territory it was—of Western Asia then occupied by the human family.

But the objections of scientists are at fault on other grounds. Geology, it is generally conceded, can tell us nothing at all about the catastrophe of which so many peoples have their traditions. And more than this: there is no certain geological evidence even of the existence of such a flood, at the time spoken of, as Moses describes.

Again, as much as the question has been discussed, it has not yet been proved that a universal flood was impossible. There are still able scientists, eminent geologists and physicists, on the affirmative as well as on the negative side of the question. Like many other questions of no practical importance, it is most likely one that will ever remain in dispute.

So much, then, for the serious (?) objections urged by our "advanced thinkers" against the teachings of the Church. When examined, they prove to be objections founded on mere assumptions or a series of assumptions—or, more truly, they are no objections at all.

What, then, about the much-vaunted conflict between Science and Religion? Is there, then, no conflict? And is Science, then, in reality the handmaid of Religion, as the defenders of revelation claim she is?

We have already answered these questions incidentally; but we deem it best to emphasize now what we have affirmed, and to state more clearly what we are to understand by Science on the one hand and the teachings of the Church on the other. As we have just seen in the difficulties we have been considering, all the objections were based on misunderstandings or misinterpretations. At most, the conflict has been one between individuals—between scientists and interpreters. This has arisen from mistaking—a common error nowadays—the theories, guesses, and vagaries of scientists for true science, for positive knowledge, for demonstrated certainties—which they are not; and from regarding the opinions, hypotheses, provisional expositions of individual theologians and commentators as the authoritative teachings of the Church.

Modern science, as it is generally spoken of—we do not refer to facts and phenomena—is at best nothing more than conjecture. There is nothing positive about it. In the language of mathematicians, it is a variable quantity; and, as we have seen, a very variable quantity it is. The theories, the explanations, the science, therefore, of to-day is abandoned for that offered to-morrow. It has been well said that modern science, as ordinarily understood, is but the opinions of the scientists of the day. How much it is a matter of conjecture is seen from the questions we have already considered. But these are not special or isolated instances. We find the same uncertainty, the same difference of opinion, in every department of science. At one time it was thought that the manifold revolutions of which geology speaks as having taken place in the earth's crust were brought about by the action of fire. At another time it was held that water was the all-powerful agent in the changes observed. Again it was supposed that the effects of upheaval and subsidence, of mountain- and continent-making, were brought about suddenly and violently, like our present volcanic eruptions and earthquakes, only that the action was on a much more stupendous scale. Now it is thought that these same effects may be accounted for by the slow operation of known causes which are still in action.

So it is with the various forces and elements with which the physicist and chemist deal. Light and heat were not long ago considered as very attenuated kinds of matter, and from the fact that they have no appreciable weight were named imponderables. Even now there are not wanting those—and this, too, among our "advanced thinkers"—who still hold to the corpuscular theory of light and heat. But there are others again, and for the nonce they are in the majority, who look upon light and heat—sound, magnetism, and electricity also—as only modes of motion, as merely different manifestations of one and the same force—a force, however, about whose real nature they are obliged to confess that they know absolutely nothing.

Again, the ordinary text-books on chemistry enumerate some sixty-five or seventy forms of matter that are called elementary—forms of matter that are incapable of decomposition, and from which all compound bodies are produced. But there are to-day—and their number is increasing—some of the ablest experimenters and most profound thinkers in chemical, physical, and astronomical science, who, for reasons that seem almost conclusive, maintain that all the so-called elements are only modifications, allotropic conditions, of one and the same primal substance.

Yet more. Just now the greatest diversity of opinion, giving rise to the most ingenious hypotheses and the most profound problems, obtain regarding the nature of matter itself.

What is matter? Are we to look upon it, as do most of the chemists of the day, as something made up of atoms of which we know nothing? Shall we, with Boscovitch and Faraday and others, regard it as nothing more than centres of force, doing away thereby with the idea of matter altogether, and reserving only that of force? Or shall we accept the latest explanation of the mystery, the vortex atom theory of Sir William Thompson and Helmholtz, who consider matter as simply rotating portions of a perfect fluid that fills all space? These are questions which not only *have not* been answered, but also questions which *cannot* be answered. Everywhere, even in apparently the simplest things, we are confronted with mysteries. And it is the speculations about these mysteries, the attempted answers of philosophers to questions proposed regarding the simplest phenomena, that we call science! Truly, there is a grave misapprehension somewhere. What is palmed off on a credulous public as science is not science, unless we choose to designate by this term the constantly changing hypotheses that are in turn offered in explanation of the facts and phenomena daily observable in the world around us.

From what we have said, however, we would not have it inferred that we are opposed to theories in science. Far from it. They often serve a useful purpose; and, as a matter of fact, if we wish to go beyond the limits of simple observation, we cannot dispense with them. But in the name of exact science, in the name of true philosophy, we do protest against the disposition, the custom, we should say, that now prevails with some of our would-be scientists, of foisting the crudest hypotheses, particularly when there is question concerning the relation between science and religion, into a place that should be reserved only for positive knowledge, for incontestable truth.

So far, we have spoken of theories only in relation to science and dogma, but we have said nothing about their bearing on politics and morals. The various theories of matter and force would at first sight seem to have little or no connection with morals or politics; and yet, as interpreted and developed by a materialistic and an atheistic philosophy, they are as intimately related as cause and effect.

Granting, with Hæckel, Straus, Vogt, and Büchner, who have no belief in a personal God, that there is nothing outside of matter and force, we can see at once what must be the logical consequences of such a premise. We could then hold, with Prof. Moleschott, that "the will is the necessary expression of a state of the brain produced by external influences. There is no such thing as free will. A crime is the logical result, direct and inevitable, of the passion which animates us. Without phosphorus, no thought." ... "Thought is a movement of matter; conscience is also a movement of matter." We could then maintain, with the German pantheist Prof. E. Von Hartmann (*Philosophy of the Unconscious*), that "it is important to make the beast-life better known to youth as being the truest source of pure nature, wherein they may learn to understand their true being in its simplest form, and in it rest and refresh themselves after the artificiality and deformity of our social condition. . . . Let us only think how *agreeably* an *ox* or a *hog* lives, almost as if he had learned to do so from Aristotle."

In speaking of Darwinism the blasphemous Hæckel observes: "Darwinism is doubtless insufficient; but that which, in spite of this, should contribute to its being admitted, is that it excludes the intervention of God. This is its inappreciable merit." Again, in speaking of his theory of morphology (as summarized in *The London Times*), he says: "In this way the Creator is disposed of, not only as superfluous, but as a Being who, if He existed, instead of being all-wise, would every now and then have committed the indiscretion of attempting to create eyes and wings which His power did not suffice to perfect." And in another place he observes: "With this simple argument the mystery of the universe is explained, Divinity is annulled, and a new era of infinite knowledge ushered in."

No wonder that Dr. Virchow—certainly no great friend of the Church—thought it time to call a halt. "Gentlemen," he says, in his address to the congress of German naturalists at Munich in 1877, "I will only hope that the evolution theory may not bring upon us all the alarm that similar theories have actually aroused in the neighboring country. At all events, this theory, if consistently carried out, has a very serious aspect, and I trust that it has not escaped your notice that Socialism has already established a sympathetic relation with it. We must not conceal these facts from ourselves." In the same address he solemnly declares: "Every attempt to transform our problems into doctrines, to introduce our hypotheses as the bases of introduction—especially the attempt simply to dispossess the Church and to supplant its dogmas forthwith by a religion of evolution,—be assured, gentlemen, every such attempt will make shipwreck, and its wreck will also bring with it the greatest perils for the whole position of science."

To the question why such pernicious doctrines as those we have just quoted should be sustained in the name of sober science, we shall let that close observer and acute thinker St. George Mivart give the answer: "A passionate hatred of religion (*Lessons from Nature*), however discreetly or astutely veiled, lies at the bottom of much of the popular metaphysical teachings now in vogue.

"A belief in the necessary inconsistency of science with religion is persistently propagated among the public by writings and lectures in which more is implied than asserted. In such lectures attempts have again and again been made to strike theology through physical science, or to blacken religion with coal-dust, or to pelt it with chalk, or to smother it with sub-Atlantic mud, or to drown it with a sea of protoplasm.

"*Delenda est Carthago.* No system is to be tolerated which will lead men to accept a personal God, moral responsibility, and a future state of rewards and punishments. Let these unwelcome truths be once eliminated, and no system is deemed undeserving of a candid, if not a sympathetic, consideration; and, *cæteris paribus*, that system which excludes the most efficaciously becomes the most acceptable."

If the doctrines which the Church proposes for our belief were as variable as, and had no better foundation than, the conjectures we are asked to accept as science; if the logical tendencies of her teachings were as disastrous in their consequences as those of popular materialistic science,—then, indeed, we should have a difficult case to plead in maintaining her position against the various so-called systems of science and philosophy that are constantly attacking her in the name of freedom of thought and intellectual advancement. Fortunately for us, such is not the case. The Church of Christ is ever the same. She teaches the same truths now as she did nineteen centuries ago, and with a certainty—because resting on Truth itself—that precludes the possibility of error. Not once in her whole history has she ever contradicted herself, or promulgated a proposition for the belief of her children that scientific investigation has proved false. In every age she has been called upon to pronounce on questions in every department of human knowledge, and her answers have been consistent both with her previous decisions and the demonstrated conclusions of science. Certainly, no one could desire a stronger proof of her divine origin, or more convincing evidence of the constant presence of the Spirit of Truth watching over her and preserving her from error. Not so with other systems of belief. The religions of Brahma and Buddha and Swedenborg are intimately mixed up with false systems of astronomy, geography, anatomy, and physiology. The latter being disproved on simple scientific grounds, the former are shown to be false. But the Catholic Church never committed herself to any theory, even when, humanly speaking, such a committal, at least in a few instances, seemed unavoidable.

"When the Copernican system," observes the learned Cardinal Newman, in his *Lectures on University Subjects*, "first made progress, what religious man would not have been tempted to uneasiness, or at least fear of scandal, from the seeming contradiction which it involved to some authoritative tradition of the Church and the declaration of Scripture? It was generally received as if the Apostles had expressly delivered it, both orally and in writing, that the earth was stationary, and that the sun was fixed in a solid firmament which whirled around the earth. After a little time, however, and on full consideration, it was found that the Church had decided next to nothing on questions such as these, and that physical science might range in this sphere of thought almost at will without fear of encountering the decisions of ecclesiastical authority. Now, besides the relief it afforded to Catholics to find that they were to be spared this addition, on the side of cosmology, to their many controversies already existing, there is something of an argument in this circumstance in behalf of the divinity of their religion. For it surely is a very remarkable fact, considering how widely and how long one certain interpretation of those physical statements in Scripture have been received by Catholics, that the Church should not have formally acknowledged it. Looking at the matter in a human point of view, it was inevitable that she should have made that opinion her own. But now we find, on ascertaining where we stand, in the face of the new sciences of these latter times, that, in spite of the bountiful comments which from the first she has ever been making on the sacred text, as it is her duty and her right to do, nevertheless she has never been led formally to explain the texts in question, or to give them an authoritative sense which modern science may question."

And yet with all this the Church has ever permitted, notwithstanding what her adversaries say to the contrary, her children the greatest liberty of thought. The latitude she allows regarding current scientific theories—we refer not to atheistic and materialistic assumptions—is a proof of our assertion. More than this. Not only has the Church permitted the greatest liberty of thought in doubtful matters of science and philosophy, or, more truly, in all matters not opposed to revealed truth, but she has also been the first to foster and stimulate, in every age, the growth of every science, and to encourage and remunerate those who distinguished themselves by their researches and discoveries.

That there is nothing in the teachings of the Church incompatible with the highest exercise of reason, that there is not a single conclusion of true science inconsistent with any article of faith, are propositions that every Catholic regards as self-evident.

The illustrious Dr. Brownson, one of the greatest philosophers that our age, or any age, has produced, says in his *Convert*, in reference to this subject: "I never in a single instance found a single article, dogma, proposition, or definition of faith which embarrassed me as a logician, or which I would, so far as my own reason was concerned, have changed or modified, or in any respect altered from what I found it, even if I had been free to do so. I have never found my reason struggling against the teachings of the Church, or felt it restrained, or myself reduced to a state of mental slavery. I have as a Catholic felt and enjoyed a mental freedom which I never conceived possible while I was a non-Catholic."

To the words of the profound Brownson—who, according to the opinion of an eminent Protestant writer, had critically examined and mastered more systems of philosophy than many persons claiming to be professors of philosophy have ever heard the names of—we may add the testimony of one who, for the depth, extent, and variety of his attainments, and for his accurate and profound knowledge in every branch of science, sacred and profane, and who, for his original researches as well as for the astonishing number of works on all subjects his prolific pen has given to the world, deserves to be called the Albertus Magnus of the nineteenth century. I refer to the illustrious Abbé Moigno of Paris, who, according to M. Dumas, Secretary of the French Academy of Sciences, when writing some years ago, " has for the last fifty years marched at the head of the scientific movement," and who is without question the first scholar of the age. In his brief autobiography prefixed to the fourth volume of his great work *Les Splendeurs de la Foi*, the learned ecclesiastic says: " I am seventy-three years old; I have read everything, I have understood everything, and I have never been troubled with the slightest doubt or temptation against faith. I have always believed, and I believe more than ever, all the truths of the Catholic, Apostolic, Roman Church, with a calm, serene, lively, strong faith, without, I repeat it, any cloud being interposed between dogma and my mind. I have sounded, as far as I have been able, all the mysteries of religion and science, and my faith has never been shaken; my voice, then, is that of an enlightened, convinced, and faithful witness."

And not less eloquent are the words of the immortal Cauchy, one of the most eminent mathematicians and physicists of modern times, and at the same time one of the most devoted and saintly sons of Mother Church. His was the honor of continuing the work of Laplace, of solving some of the most difficult problems in modern transcendental analysis, and of founding, to the glory of France, a new school of mathematical science. In his *Religious Orders* he declares: "I am a Christian; that is, I believe in the divinity of Jesus Christ, with Tycho Brahe, Copernicus, Descartes, Newton, Fermat, Leibnitz, Pascal, Grimaldi, Euler, Guldin, Boscovitch, and Gerdil, together with the great astronomers, physicists, and geometers of past ages. And, with the greater part of them, I am also a Catholic; and should any one ask me the reason, I should give it with pleasure. He would see that my convictions are not the fruit of preoccupations proceeding from birth, but the result of a most profound investigation. He would see how there have been engraved, and for ever, in my mind and heart truths that are to me more incontestible than the squaring of the hypotheneuse or the theorem of Maclaurin. I am a sincere Catholic, as were Corneille, Racine, La Bruyère, Bossuet, Bourdaloue, and Fenelon; as have been, and are, many of the most distinguished men of our day, who have done honor to science, philosophy, and literature, and added lustre to our academies more than all others besides. I share the profound convictions manifested in the works, discourses, and lives of so many *savants* of the first order: of the Ruffinis, the Haüys, the Laënnecs, the Ampères, the Pelletiers, the Freycinets, the Cariolis. And if I name not those who still live, fearing lest I should wound their modesty, I can at least say that it has always been most grateful to me to meet all the nobility and all the generosity of Christian faith in my illustrious friends: in the founder of crystallography; in the discoverer of quinine; in the inventor of the stethoscope; and in the immortal author of dynamical electricity."

But this is sufficient. We shall make a brief summary of what we have said, and conclude. We have seen, then, that all real scientific discoveries only go to corroborate the doctrines that the Church proposes for our acceptance. We have learned that the so-called conflict between Science and Religion is a conflict between private individuals—scientists and philosophers with their hypotheses, on the one hand, commentators and theologians with their provisional interpretations, on the other. We have found, too, that the most prominent scientific theories of the day, aside from the consequences falsely deduced from them, are perfectly reconcilable with Catholic dogma; that the Catholic student enjoys the greatest possible liberty of thought in matters of science and speculation; and that the Church, far from impeding his progress, true to her divine mission and true to her past history, is the first to encourage and assist him.

The Church has nothing to fear from scientific progress, but much to gain. Every new conquest of science is a new argument in the natural order confirmatory of the verities that God has been pleased to reveal. No one can have greater reason to rejoice at the advance of science than the Church, for she is conscious that every acquisition of science will be an addition to her sacred treasure of heavenly, divine truth. Science is the handmaid of Religion. Between true science and true religion, between modern science—in so far as it is science—and the Catholic Church, a conflict not only does not exist, but is not even possible. Both point in the same direction; both should lead us to the Author of all good—God, our Father.

CHAPTER II.

CATHOLIC SCIENTISTS AND THEIR ACHIEVEMENTS.

"The Church, far from being opposed to the progress of human arts and sciences, assists and encourages them in many ways."—*Constitution of the Vatican Council.*

"The sceptre of Science belongs to Christian Europe."—*Count de Maistre.*

THE illustrious Count Joseph de Maistre declares that "history, during the last three hundred years, has been a grand conspiracy against the truth." And we might to-day reiterate this statement as emphatically as did the learned author when he stood before the world as the champion of truth and religion. History, since the period of the so-called Reformation, has been perverted, and hence the many charges one continually sees preferred against the Church whenever there is question of her relation to the world of thought and intellectual advancement. She has been decried as the enemy of liberty and civilization, and yet it is to her that we are indebted for both. She has been declared inimical to the progress of art and literature, albeit the greatest masterpieces in every department of literature and art are the immediate result of her inspiration and fostering care. She has been proclaimed the open enemy of science; and notwithstanding all that has been done during the last fifty years in every department of historical inquiry, showing how groundless such an accusation is, the impression is still abroad that the Church has always been opposed to science, and has ever, during her entire history, strenuously and systematically discouraged its study and contravened its progress. But this impression, although originally due to a falsifying of the facts of history, is now a result rather of the declamations and diatribes pronounced against the Church by those of our modern "advanced thinkers" whose systems she has condemned as opposed to true philosophy, and whose science she has sifted and declared to contain nothing more than the chaff of theory and fanciful speculation. There is, then, no more truth in the charge that the Church has been inimical to scientific advancement than that she is opposed to liberty and civilization, or to the cultivation of art and literature.

As a matter of fact, it would be less difficult, in the light of authentic history, to tell what the Church has not done for science than to state what she has done. To tell what the Church has done would be to write the history of every branch of science—to follow each branch from its first beginnings to the highly developed state to which it has attained. It would prove, and prove beyond quirk or quibble, the beautiful statement of the Count de Maistre, whom we have just quoted, that "the sceptre of Science belongs to Christian Europe." It would demonstrate, and demonstrate without peradventure, the truth of those admirable words of the fourth chapter of the dogmatic constitution of the Vatican Council, that "the Church, far from being opposed to the progress of human arts and sciences, assists and encourages them in many ways;" that "she is not ignorant of, and does not despise, the advantages which accrue from them to the life of mankind;" and that "she does more, and recognizes that, coming from God, the Author of science, their proper use should, with the assistance of His grace, lead to God."

These words of De Maistre and of the Vatican Council may, then, in a way, serve as our thesis, as they embody, in a great measure, all that we shall have to say on the subject. We shall endeavor to show that the sceptre of Science truly belongs to the Church by every title on which it is possible to base a claim—that history declares it, that the facts maintain it.

We shall, in the first place, call attention to the fact that the great universities of Europe are Catholic in their origin, and that most of them were founded long before the period of the Reformation. We shall then show that Catholic students were the first to introduce the true system in the study of nature—that of observation and experiment, and known as the method of induction—and that they had employed it, and with success, centuries before the time of Lord Bacon, its alleged originator. We shall next see—and we specify it in advance, as we wish it to constitute the most salient feature of our article—how eminently practical the children of the Church have been always in all their studies and investigations; for, as we proceed, we shall discover that all the great discoveries and inventions that have exerted the most potent influence in advancing scientific knowledge and in ameliorating the condition of our race are to be credited to the Church and to her devoted children. In reconnoitring the vast domain of nature, their aim has always been, as we shall notice, to observe and classify the various facts and phenomena which presented themselves in answer to inquiries, and to eschew theory and hypothesis except when of evident assistance in co-ordinating and systematizing the results of their researches. And, finally, after recounting what the Church has done directly through her children, we shall consider what she has done indirectly by her influence—an influence which, it will be found, has been as efficacious in forwarding the cause of science as it has been in contributing to the advance of civilization. In a word, we shall find that the Church, during the whole course of her history, has always moved forward. In the world of thought she has never stood still nor retrograded; and much less has she retarded in any way the grand intellectual march of mankind, ever seeking new conquests in the boundless realms of nature and science.

If we take up the annals of science, we shall find that the pioneers and most active and successful workers in every branch thereof have not only been devoted sons of the Church, but also, in many instances, have been, and still are, ecclesiastics and members of religious orders. We shall, as we proceed, give the names of some of these, and state what they have accomplished; but, for want of space, we shall be obliged to pass over many names and discoveries that have reflected glory on the Church of God as well as on their authors. If we can succeed in exciting in the minds of our readers an interest in the subject and a desire for further information—which they can obtain by going over at their leisure the history of science—we shall feel that our efforts have not been in vain.

Every student of history knows that the great universities of Europe were founded by Catholic kings and princes, and often under immediate Papal inspiration. Away back in the Middle Ages, and long before the appearance of the Reformation, Oxford and Cambridge, Aberdeen and St. Andrews, Upsala and Copenhagen, Paris,

Toulouse, and Montpelier, Leipsic, Heidelberg, Tübingen, Wurzburg, Cracow, Prague, Vienna, Bologna, Naples, Pisa, Turin, Rome, Salamanca, Seville, Valladolid, Coimbra, Louvain, were celebrated seats of learning, and attended by thousands of students. In some instances the number exceeded 10,000 for one university—something unknown in modern times—and this, too, centuries before Luther rose up in rebellion against the Church, and sounded that note of discord that almost destroyed the social and intellectual harmony of Christian Europe.

In these centres of intellectual activity genius had full play, and the mind, untrammelled in its operations, was free to range over the entire realm of thought, and to enter every department of knowledge, sacred and profane. Here were taught all the branches of art and science; here we find the first beginnings of many of those discoveries which, with subsequent development, have excited the admiration of a wondering world; and here, to quote Carlyle, "nearly all the inventions and civil institutions whereby we yet live as civilized men were originated and perfected."

We have said that it is to the schools and scholars of mediæval Europe that we owe the inductive or experimental method of study which has contributed so materially to the advancement of natural and physical science. We owe it, among others, to Gerbert, afterward Pope Sylvester II.—born A. D. 920; died 1003—who was reputed to be the greatest scholar of his age; to Albertus Magnus, that towering genius of the 13th century, and to his great contemporary Roger Bacon. We know that the earl of Verulam, Lord Bacon, has been claimed as the originator of the inductive system of philosophy; but any one who has read aught of the history of science knows full well that the system was accepted and followed hundreds of years before Lord Bacon was born.

Far back in the 13th century the illustrious Dominican friar Albertus Magnus writes, in one of his works: "All that is here set down is the result of my own experience, or has been borrowed from authors whom we know to have written what their personal experience has confirmed; for in these matters experience alone can give certainty."

Roger Bacon, an English monk of the Order of the seraphic St. Francis d'Assisi, was so far in advance of his age that the erudite historian of *The Inductive Sciences*, Dr. Whewell, declares that "it is difficult to conceive how such a character could then exist." Speaking of one of the works of the learned friar, the *Opus Majus*, he remarks: "I regard the existence of such a work as the *Opus Majus* at that period as a problem that has never yet been solved." Continuing, he says: "It is indeed an extraordinary circumstance to find a writer of the 13th century not only recognizing experiment as one of the sources of knowledge, but urging its claims as something far more important than men had yet been aware of, exemplifying its value by striking and just examples, and speaking of its authority with a dignity of diction which sounds like a forerunner of the Baconian sentences uttered four hundred years later. Yet this is the character of what we find." He then quotes the following paragraph from the *Opus Majus* of the doctor mirabilis: "Experimental science, the sole mistress of speculative sciences, has three great prerogatives among other parts of knowledge: first, she tests by experiment the noblest conclusions of all other sciences; next, she discovers, respecting the notions which other sciences deal with, magnificent truths to which those other sciences of themselves can by no means attain; her third dignity is that she, by her own power and without respect of other sciences, investigates the secrets of nature."

W. Stanley Jevons, in his admirable *Principles of Science*, speaking of the work of Lord—not Friar—Bacon, says: "It is a great mistake to say modern science is the result of the Baconian philosophy. He mistook the true mode of using experience, and, in attempting to apply his method, ridiculously failed. Whether we look to Galileo, who preceded Bacon, to Gilbert, his contemporary, or to Newton and Descartes, Leibnitz and Huygens, his successors, we find that discovery was achieved by the very opposite method to that advocated by Bacon."

J. W. Draper, whom no one will accuse of being partial to Catholic interests, attributes the great work of reform in the methods of scientific investigation to that universal genius of the fifteenth century, Leonardo da Vinci. "To him, and not to Lord Bacon, must be attributed the renaissance of science. Bacon was not only ignorant of mathematics, but depreciated its application to physical inquiries. He contemptuously rejected the Copernican system, alleging absurd objections against it. While Galileo was on the brink of his great telescopic discoveries Bacon was publishing doubts as to the utility of instruments in scientific investigations. To ascribe the inductive method to him is to ignore history. His fanciful philosophical suggestions have never been of the slightest practical use. No one has ever thought of employing them. Except among English readers, his name is almost unknown."

We quote these passages, and dwell thus at length on the point to which they relate, because we wish to show that Catholic scientists were not only acute observers and industrious investigators, but that to them is due the inductive method that is now universally employed in scientific research. This is important. It is claimed as one of the great glories of a later age, but, as we have seen, without foundation. Introduced by the monks of the Middle Ages, and continued by their successors, it was later on employed by the professors of science in the universities of Italy and other countries, until the time of Galileo and his school, when it may be said to have reached its culmination.

It was by studying in accordance with the principles of the inductive philosophy—by insisting on experiment—that mediæval and modern scholars have been able to make such giant strides in natural and physical science. Laying aside the speculative and metaphysical systems of the Greek and Alexandrian schools, and questioning nature directly, Galileo and his pupils, many of them ecclesiastics, were able to accomplish more in a few years than the philosophers of Greece and Rome had achieved during the long intellectual ascendency of their respective countries. During the six hundred years that the schools of Athens were open, less of actual work was done in physical science than Galileo, unaided and alone, accomplished in a lifetime. The difference in the result was due—we repeat it—wholly and solely to the method employed by the Italian philosopher—a method for which Galileo was indebted to the monks of the Middle Ages no less than to his own transcendent genius.

From what we have just said it is evident that our estimate of the alleged "Dark Ages" must be quite different from the one which is so frequently given. This period of time was not only an age of faith, but, to borrow the words of Ruskin in a recent lecture, "an age which was eminently productive of, eminently under the governance and guidance of, men of the widest and most brilliant faculties, constructive and speculative—men whose acts had become the romance, whose thoughts the wisdom, and whose arts the treasure, of a thousand years."

We have shown that we are indebted to the sons of Holy Church for the correct system of scientific study. Can it likewise be proved that we owe anything to them for the application of this system to actual and successful work? In other words, have Catholic scientists been distinguished for any important inventions or discoveries, or anything that should entitle them to the lasting gratitude of their race? Yes: and these are the questions that we now purpose answering by recounting, as briefly as may be, some of the more important contributions made to science by Catholic scientists working under Catholic influences, and often, too, in an age and in countries distinctively Catholic.

Let us commence with geography, the science which teaches us concerning the earth on which we live. Has it ever occurred to our readers that nearly all the knowledge we have of the earth's surface comes to us from Catholic sources? Far back in the sixth century we have an Egyptian monk, the learned cosmographer Cosmas Indicopleustes, who, according to Malte-Brun, a competent critic surely, was the author of the only original work of that epoch, and who as a geographer was scarcely less worthy of consideration than Ptolemy. After him came the missionaries of the gospel, who, at the command of the Popes, went on their errands of charity to parts of the world until then unknown, and on their return gave the people of Europe a knowledge of the countries which they had visited. In 1246, Father John de Piano Carpino, accompanied by some Franciscan monks, was sent by Innocent IV. to Kuyak Khan, the emperor of Tartary, and journeyed as far as Thibet. In 1253, Father Rubruquis, another Franciscan, went, by order of Louis IX. of France, in search of Prester John, and penetrated farther into Asia than had any other European before his time. These two apostolic friars, together with Ascelin, also a missionary, are, according to the testimony of Malte-Brun, as deserving of the eternal gratitude of geographers as are the Columbuses and Cooks of a later age. They stimulated others to explore unknown lands, and thus contributed greatly to the advancement of geographical knowledge. Sir John Mandeville, the celebrated English traveller of the 13th century, Vasco de Gama, and even Columbus, were indebted to them for much information in their journeys and voyages of exploration.

But the grandest discoveries in the Orient at this period were made by the illustrious Venetian traveller Marco Polo, whom the great geographer Malte-Brun pronounces the Humboldt of the thirteenth century. Going with his father, uncle, and a few monks to the Pope to receive the pontiff's blessing, they set out in 1271 for the court of Kublai Khan, the Tartar conqueror of China. After a journey of more than three years they reached a city near the present site of Pekin. After residing twenty-four years in the East, travelling much of the time, Marco Polo returned to his home, and wrote an account of his travels which first made known to the people of Europe the existence of many of the countries and islands of the East, including Japan.

It was Columbus, sailing under the banner of the Cross, who discovered the New World; Vasco de Gama, carrying a flag on which was the cross of the military order of the Most Holy Redeemer, who first doubled the Cape of Good Hope and reached the East Indies; Magellan, following the cross and the standard of Castile, who first rounded Cape Horn; and, although he did not get any farther than the Philippine Islands, where he met his death at the hands of the natives, his ship, the "Santa Victoria," continued her journey, and, going by way of the East Indies and the Cape of Good Hope, was the first to effect the circumnavigation of the globe. Cortez and Balboa and their associates explored Mexico and Central America; Pizarro and his countrymen, the unknown lands of South America; and De Soto, the territory bordering the northern portion of the Gulf of Mexico.

The sons of Catholic France went to Canada and what is now called British America, and made known to their brethren in Europe the countries they had visited and the manners and customs of their inhabitants. La Salle and Father Marquette, a Jesuit; Hennepin and Membré, Franciscans, explored the great chain of lakes from Ontario to Superior, and the lands and tribes adjacent, and were the first to journey from the source to the mouth of the Father of Waters. We have only to look over the maps of the different countries of the world to recognize the handwriting of the children of Holy Church. Everywhere, in spite of the many changes in names that have been introduced by writers and map-makers of a later age, we find cities, countries, islands, lakes, and rivers bearing names that could have been suggested only by Catholic hearts and souls ever mindful of the glory of their Church and of her saints, and of the grandeur of the doctrines and mysteries which she inculcates.

The discoverers of the mainland of North America were John and Sebastian Cabot; the discoverer of Lower Canada and the river St. Lawrence was James Cartier; the discoverer of

Lake Huron was the Franciscan Joseph le Caron; the discoverer of lakes Champlain and Ontario, and the founder of Quebec, was Samuel de Champlain; the founders of the oldest cities in the United States, Santa Fé and St. Augustine, were Oñate and Menendez; the founder of San Francisco and the apostle of California was Junipero Serra. The first maps of lakes Ontario and Superior were made by the Jesuits, and are found in their *Relations;* the first map of Lake Erie was drawn by the Sulpician Dollier de Casson. The salt springs of Onondaga were discovered by a Jesuit; and the oil-wells near Lake Erie by a Franciscan. And thus we might detail at length the achievements of the sons of the Church. We trace their footsteps from Vinland, discovered by Lief Ericson and his Catholic Northmen, to far-off Alaska, the scene of the explorations and labors of the sainted Archbishop Seghers. On every page of the history of our country Catholic explorers, missionaries, and scholars have left their imprint. Verrazzano, Ponce de Leon, Pineta, Gomez, Miruelo, Ayllon, Gordillo, Tristan de Luna, Coronado Castañada, Du Lhut, Joliet, White, Sir George Calvert, Lord Baltimore—Catholics all of them—are but a few that might be named of the long list of those who by their achievements have reflected honor on Church and country.

The Western Hemisphere is named after Amerigo Vespucci, a Catholic navigator, who visited the New World shortly after Columbus. The first map of any value of the great Empire of China, the "Atlas de la Chine," was made by Jesuit priests. And generations before the times of Burton, Speke, Livingstone, and Stanley, the tribes of Central Africa had witnessed the labors of the missionary who had come to bring them the glad tidings of the gospel. Only a few years ago the attention of the scientific world was called to a terrestrial globe in Lyons, France, that long before had been constructed by the Franciscan fathers, which showed many geographical features whose discovery had been credited to modern explorers.

Among the contemporary explorers of the "Dark Continent" is the well-known French ecclesiastic, Abbé Debaize. And among those who have specially been honored in late years for their contributions to geographical knowledge is Father Desgidius, the learned explorer of the frontiers of Thibet, and Father Petitot, who has recently been made the recipient of a gold medal for his geographical labors in Alaska, as has also been the Lazarist missionary David, for his researches on the geography and natural history of China. But let us turn from what the sons of the Church have done for the advancement of the science of geography—for we might go on indefinitely telling of what they have achieved in this field—to what they have done for astronomy.

It was Dionysius the Little, a Roman monk, who, in the middle of the sixth century, introduced the system of chronology that obtained in Europe for upward of a thousand years. The famous Gerbert and Friar Bacon were the great astronomical lights of the tenth and thirteenth centuries. Indeed, nearly every astronomer of note for the first fifteen centuries of the Church's history was an ecclesiastic. It was Nicholas of Cusa, afterward cardinal, who first called attention to the weakness of the Ptolemaic system, which makes the earth the centre of the universe; but it was reserved for the great Copernicus, an humble Polish priest, to develop the system that has since borne his name—a system which makes the sun, and not the earth, the centre of the solar system. And, contrary to the generally received impression, the first to accept and promulgate the new doctrine were the dignitaries of the Church and the professors of the Catholic univerities of Europe. The great work *De Orbium Cælestium Revolutionibus*, in which Copernicus worked out his theory, was published at the instance of Cardinal Schomberg and Bishop Tiedman Giese, and dedicated to the then reigning Pontiff, Paul III. The learned Jesuit Christopher Clavius defended it in Germany; the Augustinian friar Diego de Zuñiga proclaimed it in Spain; and the Carmelite Foscarina supported it in Italy; whilst the learned Cardinal Barbarini, afterward Pope Urban VIII., the great advocate of arts and letters, gave it his patronage in Rome, which was then the centre of science as well as of Christendom.

But mark those who were most violent in their opposition to the new system. Lord Bacon, the alleged father of experimental science, never accepted it. Tycho Brahé, the Danish astronomer, preferred a theory of his own—an awkward and complicated one, based on that of Ptolemy. Both ridiculed the heliocentric theory, and heaped opprobrious epithets on its author. Melancthon called the new doctrine an absurdity, and referred to it as the production of an imbecile or of one who was striving to gain notoriety. Luther, the vaunted champion of intellectual freedom, spoke of Copernicus as "an upstart astrologer, who strives to show that the earth revolves—not the heavens, nor the firmanent, nor the sun, nor the moon. Whoever wishes to appear clever must devise some new system, which, of all systems, is of course the very best. This fool wishes to reverse the entire science of astronomy."

The annals of astronomy in subsequent times tell the same story. Those who contributed most to the advance of astronomical science—those who achieved most marked distinction for their brilliant discoveries—were Catholics. It was Galileo Galilei, about whom so many romances have been written—Galileo, the friend and *protégé* of cardinals and popes, who, imaginative historians would have us believe, were his persecutors—who invented the telescope, which, with a few discoveries he soon made, entirely revolutionized the science of astronomy. It was he who discovered the satellites of Jupiter, the ring of Saturn, the mountains of the moon, the spots on the sun, and the rotation of this luminary on its axis. He also resolved the Milky Way into myriads of stars, observed the phases of the planet Venus, and made known the moon's diurnal libration. And here let us call the attention of the reader to the fact that Galileo made some of these observations in the Quirinal gardens belonging to his friend and patron Cardinal Bandini. There he had placed his telescope, and there, all statements to the contrary notwithstanding, he met with that favor and encouragement which spurred his genius on to other discoveries and more brilliant achievements. And let us also observe that Galileo recieved a life pension in order to be able to prosecute his studies, and that the one who granted this pension was one who, we are seriously told, was among his persecutors—the great Pope Urban VIII.

Galileo's scholars, Cassini, Maraldi, Castelli, and Bianchini, carried on his work in astronomy as well as in the other branches of physical science. The famous Abbé Gassendi was the first to observe a transit of Mercury over the sun's disc and to determine its diameter. Piazzi, a Theatine monk, discovered Ceres, the first of the asteroids. He also prepared a catalogue of seven thousand stars, so perfect in all its observations that only a few decades ago Prof. Airy, late astronomer Royal of England, spoke of it "as referred to by all observers as a standard catalogue," and "as the greatest work undertaken by any modern astronomer." To this same Piazzi, Lalande declared astronomy owed more than to any man since the great Greek observer Hipparchus. A priest, Orioli, was the first to determine the orbit of the planet Uranus; and the first to add the telescope to the quadrant, and to make the first exact measure of the earth's meridian, was a learned French ecclesiastic, the Abbé Picard, first president of the French Academy of Sciences. This latter work of his, the measurement of the earth's meridian, may not, at first sight, appear to be of much consequence, and yet it is to it directly—we may say solely—that we owe Newton's great law of universal gravitation. Newton had long worked on the subject, but with unsatisfactory results. Twenty years later, he was made acquainted with the result of Picard's measurements, and resumed the calculations he had so long abandoned, when lo! thanks to the French abbé's achievement, the problem of universal gravitation, so wide-reaching in its importance, was solved.

Neptune, the most distant planet of the solar system, was discovered by Leverrier, and in a way that will make him rank for all time to come with the greatest of mathematicians and the most profound of astronomers. Observing that the path of the planet Uranus deviated from that traced out by mathematicians, he went to work and calculated, from the observed irregularities of the planet's motion in her orbit, not only the size and orbit of the disturbing body, which neither he nor any one else had ever seen, but actually pointed out the place the planet should occupy in the heavens at a given time. The telescope was turned to that point, and for the first time was visible to human eyes the planet Neptune. And who was Leverrier? He was the director of the French National Observatory. But he was something more: he was a devout Catholic. In the observatory he had two objects he was always wont to point to with pride: his grand refracting telescope—the finest then in the world—and his crucifix; two objects that, to his mind, were typical of what can not be too closely united—Science and Religion.

To the learned Jesuit De Vico, the discoverer of eight comets, whose observations and calculations have stamped him as one of the ablest astronomers of any age; to Father Secchi, recognized everywhere as the greatest authority on the sun and its constitution, and one of the foremost investigators in that important branch of modern astronomy, spectrum analysis; and to Father

Perry, the late director of the observatory at Stonyhurst, we are indebted as much, if not more, for contributions to the advancement of astronomical knowledge as to any other three men of the present century.

We should like to mention others who have equally honored astronomy and the Church, but the list is too long to admit of their being noticed with any justice. Suffice it to say that it was the religious orders of the Church—and notably the Benedictines, Jesuits, and Augustinians—that first gave an impetus to the erection of observatories and to the dissemination of astronomical knowledge among the masses. Before they took the matter in hand telescopes and astronomical appliances were to be found only in large cities. But after these learned religious commenced their work, observatories were to be found wherever they had a school or college; and many of the best-known observatories of Europe to-day are, like her great universities, to be credited to the work or direct influence of the Church. Rome, Florence, Venice, Milan, Parma, Avignon, Lyons, Lisbon, Marseilles, Vienna, Wurzburg, Manheim, Gratz, Prague, Breslau, Posen, and other places in Europe owed to the illustrious orders just named their first observatories. To these same orders is due the credit of being the first to found observatories in other parts of the world—in the capitals and larger towns of South America, in the Phillipine Islands, in Australia, and in their various missions in the East Indies and China. It is well known that the Jesuits on entering China not only carried with them the gospel, but all the instruments for the successful study of the science of astronomy, and that in the year 1620 they replaced the natives in the management of the observatories of the Celestial Empire. It would seem that these zealous missionaries wished to show their superiority in the knowledge of the visible as well as of the invisible universe, in order the more easily to draw the minds of their hearers to a study of that which is eternal, and to the knowledge of a heaven more beautiful and more lasting than that which affords such delight to the mortal eye of the astronomer.

Ecclesiastics, too, have been frequently called on as the most competent persons to make important observations in foreign parts when special skill and knowledge were required. In 1760, Juan Chappe d'Auteroche, a French priest, was delegated by the Academy of Sciences of Paris to observe the transit of Venus in Tobolsk, Siberia, and a few years later he was sent on a similar expedition to California, his efforts in both instances being crowned with the most flattering success. Similarly, Father Alexander Guy was chosen by the same Academy to observe the transit of Venus in the Indian Ocean; and he did his work so well that he was subsequently called upon several times to execute other important commissions in the interests of navigation and astronomy. In our own day, Father Perry, S. J., has been sent on a similar expedition by the English Government to Kerguelen, Madagascar, and South America. One of the most eminent astronomers of Italy to-day is Padre Denza, a Barnabite monk, who is the director of the Vatican observatory, reconstructed and equipped by the munificence of our Holy Father, Leo XIII. In all parts of the world ecclesiastics now have charge of observatories— at Rome, Louvain, Puebla, Havana, Kalosca, Calcutta, Zikawei, Tchang-kia-Tchouang in China, Georgetown and Washington, D. C., and numerous other places—and the value of their work, performed quietly and unostentatiously, is known and appreciated only by those who are capable of judging of the merits of accurate study and delicate observations.

The Church has invariably taken the lead in mathematical discovery and development. Arithmetic as a science owes its origin in Europe to the learned Gerbert. The first work on algebra was published in Venice in 1494 by a Franciscan friar, Paccioli di Borgo. He went as far as equations of the second degree, and foresaw the application of algebra to geometry. His book served as the basis of all the works on algebra written during the succeeding century. Paccioli's work was developed by George Reisch, prior of the Carthusian monastery at Freiburg. Cavalieri, of the order of Jeromites, was one of the inventors of the infinitesimal calculus, and solved many problems that Kepler and other eminent mathematicians had given up in despair. He made known the relations between the spiral and the parabola, and worked out the great problem of Kepler concerning the revolution of a parabola about its ordinate. He wrote the first approach to a treatise on the conic sections. His work on *Continuous Indivisibles* paved the way for the great mathematical triumphs of Leibnitz and Newton. The quadrature of the circle and other puzzling problems were solved by the Jesuit Gregory de San Vicenté. Father Mersenne, of the order of Minims, and the intimate friend of Descartes, was the inventor of the cycloid. The cyclo-cylindrical curve is the invention of Father Laloubère. Ferrari of Bologna discovered equations of the fourth degree. Father Christopher Grinberger was the first to develop central projections, or the projection of a sphere on a plane surface. And so we might continue to enumerate the works of other ecclesiastics who did much for the development of all the branches of mathematical science—Boscovich, Maco, Riccati, and Moigno, Jesuits; Lesueur and Jacquier, Franciscans; Inniger, Sadler, and Maurer, Augustinians; and hosts of others whose names are inscribed in the history of science.

Besides the ecclesiastics just referred to, we

might mention a long list among the laity who have been as devoted to the Church as they were to science. We shall, however, content ourselves with the names of Pascal, Cauchy, Adrianus Romanus, Descartes, and Hermite, the last mentioned of whom is acknowledged to be the foremost of living mathematicians. Pascal was the first to approach the binomial theorem of Newton, and to lay down the principles of the calculation of probabilities; and, according to Laplace, he was, with Fermat, one of the chief inventors of the differential calculus. Cauchy was celebrated as the greatest mathematician and analyst of his time, and is distinguished among mathematicians for his contributions to analysis and the residuary and imaginary calculus. Adrien van Roomen, or Adrianus Romanus, as he is generally called, a professor of the University of Louvain during the latter part of the sixteenth century, was one of the ablest mathematicians of his age. His is the glory of having invented modern or symbolical algebra, a work which was more fully developed by the French geometer Viète. Before his time the operations of algebra, besides being comparatively limited in their applications, were carried on in ordinary language—a process that was as long as it was complicated. The introduction of letters and symbols by Romanus, and the subsequent additions by Viète, gave us algebra as we have it to-day—universal in its application to quantities of what kind soever, be they the numbers of arithmetic or the figures of geometry. Descartes holds a conspicuous place with the master minds of history. He was the inventor of the new geometry, which consists in the application of algebra to geometry—a discovery which, to quote a well-known French author, "by its facility, uniformity, and the generality of its rules, cast at once into the shade all the geometrical theories of the ancients, and became for two centuries the almost exclusive instrument in researches on the properties of space." It has, according to the illustrious French mathematician Michel Chasles, "changed the face of the science of mathematics, and may to-day be regarded as the invention which has most contributed toward its progress." Indeed, it was by arming themselves with this method that Fermat, Pascal, Sulze, Roberval, Leibnitz, and Newton were enabled to create a still more powerful instrument, the infinitesimal calculus, to which we are indebted for the rapid and immense progress made in our knowledge of the heavenly bodies and in the laws of mechanics and physics.

We should like also to tell of the work of the pious Michel Chasles, of whom it was said by a contemporary mathematician that all the geometers of Europe were his disciples—of that Chasles of whose work the eminent physicist Sir E. Sabine did not hesitate to say: "If one considers the vast extent of the field thus opened to our investigations, it is very probable that, considered as an instrument of research in pure geometry, the method of M. Chasles may bear comparison with any discovery of the present century." We should like, too, to tell of other ornaments of mathematical science—of Biot, Puisieux, of Gaspar Monge, the assistant of Abbé Nollet, and, later on, the inventor of descriptive geometry; but we must hurry on.

In the various departments of physics we are again indebted to children of the Church for not only taking the initiative, but also for placing the landmarks of the science. It was Leonardo da Vinci, and subsequently Galileo and his school—Torricelli, Vivianni, Borelli, Castelli, Mersenne, and Gassendi, the last three of whom were ecclesiastics—who created those branches of the science known as mechanics, hydrostatics, hydraulics, and hydro-dynamics. They were the first to cast aside the traditions of the ancients, and to substitute experiment for the dicta of Aristotle and the teachers of the Alexandrian school. Before Galileo's time little was known about the laws of solids and fluids in motion. But the scholars just mentioned took the matter in hand, and performed their work so well that they left comparatively little for subsequent investigators to accomplish. Many of their experiments are yet classical, and the wonder is how sciences like those just mentioned could be created and almost fully developed in such a short time.

And yet all this work was done in the shadow of the Church, and much of it by monks. And so also in every branch of physics we shall find laws and apparatus bearing the names of ecclesiastics. Castelli, the pupil and co-laborer of Galileo, distinguished for his investigations in mechanics, and called by Montucla "the creator of a new branch of hydraulics," was a Benedictine. Mariotte, famed for his researches in pneumatics, was a Premonstratensian and the prior of a French monastery. Even the well-known experiment of the guinea and feather in a tube exhausted of air was devised by him. Mersenne, to whom we have referred as a mathematician, but who also made many discoveries in acoustics, was a religious of the order of Minims. Indeed, so numerous and important were Mersenne's experiments and discoveries in the domain of sound that he is justly styled the "Father of Acoustics." Grimaldi, known for his experiments on the interference of light, to which phenomena he was the first to direct attention, and Secchi, the inventor of the automatic meteorograph, so important to meteorologists, were members of the Society of Jesus. The first to use a convex lens in the telescope was Schyrle de Rheita, a Capuchin. He was also the inventor of the double telescope, better known as the opera-glass. Nollet, famous for his experiments in static electricity, and Caselli, the inventor of the wonderful pantelegraph, were also ecclesiastics. The Archbishop Spalatro de Dominis was the first to give a true explanation of the rainbow. Away back in 1626, a hundred and fifty years before Watt's time, Father Leurochon published a work entitled *Récréations Mathématiques*, in which he treated at length of the power of steam and of the practical application of steam-motors. About fifty years later, the Abbé Hautefeuille took up the same subject, and discussed also a machine to be actuated by explosives—a machine that afterward so much engaged the attention of Papin, and which has culminated in our modern gas-engine. Fathers Galien and Lana were the first to tackle experimentally the subject of aërial navigation; and the Abbé Moüger, Desforges, and the learned Benedictine Oliver of Malmesbury were the first to construct what are now considered as matters of recent invention, and what are at present exciting such universal interest in both Europe and America—flying machines.

Of more recent investigators among the clergy who have distinguished themselves for their original work, we might mention Fathers Panceni, Zantedeschi, and Carbonelle, who are known for their researches on heat and light; Canon Lalande, celebrated for his experiments in static electricity; and that prodigy of science the late lamented Abbé Moigno of Paris. But the list of ecclesiastics who have made a name for themselves by their contributions to physical science is already sufficiently long.

If we turn to the laity, we find that the number of those whom the Church as well as Science counts as her own is still greater. Of these, however, we can name but a few; and we call attention to them especially because it is so rarely that justice is done them or that their contributions to the advance of physical science are recognized. In many cases, indeed, they are comparatively unknown, and their discoveries and inventions are credited to others. It is asserted, for instance, that the microscope was invented by a German, Jansen of Middlebury, in 1619; and yet it is a fact of history that Galileo had presented one of his own invention to the king of Poland seven years before. Of course, as one may well understand, the microscope, as then constructed, was far from being comparable with those admirable instruments possessed by the microscopists of to-day. But still the principle of the instrument was the same, and the glory of the invention belongs without question to Galileo.

J. B. Fourier, who spent some years in a Benedictine monastery, and who entertained serious thoughts of donning the habit of St. Benedict, is famous among scientists for his great work on *The Mathematical Theory of Heat*—a work that still serves as a guide to the most eminent physicists and mathematicians of the day in their investigations concerning the properties and laws of heat, especially as manifested in the phenomena of radiation and conduction. Fourier, together with his countrymen and contemporaries Regnault, Dulong, and Petit, have probably contributed more than any four men of the present century toward establishing the laws of heat and placing the subject on a scientific basis.

Descartes was the first to discover the laws of the refraction of light, and, according to French writers, was also the first to show the composition of the solar ray. Malus and Fresnel were the first to develop the subject of the polarization of light, as Fizeau and Foucault were the first to determine, by apparatus constructed for that purpose, the velocity of light. It was Foucault also, one of the greatest of modern mechanicians, who invented many appliances now deemed indispensable in the study of astronomy and physics. He was the inventor of those wonders of mechanical ingenuity, the heliostat, siderostat, automatic electric arc lamp, and silvered reflectors. He was also the first to show in a palpable manner the rotation of the earth on its axis by his wonderful experiment with the pendulum, which he suspended from the dome of the Panthéon in Paris, and by that beautiful instrument he afterward invented in illustration of the same fact—the gyroscope.

We are indebted to Galvani for the discovery

of dynamical electricity; to Volta for the first battery; and to Nobili and Melloni for some of the most important and delicate instruments to be found in our modern laboratories—viz. the galvanometer, the thermo-electric multiplier, and accessory apparatus. The one to raise the subject of dynamo-electricity to the dignity of a science was Ampère, a man as remarkable for his ardent faith as he was for his great knowledge of science. Nearly all the apparatus now used for the illustration of the laws of electro-magnetism were devised by this distinguished savant. Indeed, so thoroughly did he accomplish his work that he left little to be done by those who came after him. And the torsion balance—an instrument that is indispensable in all accurate and delicate measurements of slight forces, especially of magnetism and electricity—is the invention of the French physicist Coulomb, who, according to Whewell, was one of the most eminent physical philosophers of the last century.

After having told what the sons of the Church have done for physics, it would be superfluous to state that they have achieved fully as much for chemistry. These two branches of science are in some respects so intimately associated that their progress must be more or less uniform and simultaneous. During the Middle Ages, and even subsequently, their most successful and assiduous cultivators were members of the monastic orders. Any one at all conversant with the history of chemistry knows that it is to the alchemists of the Middle Ages that we owe many of the appliances still used in our laboratories. Some of the most important acids, bases, and salts were the results of their researches and the products of their experiments while seeking for the universal solvent, the philosopher's stone, and the elixir of life. We are now disposed to underrate their work because they were searching for what we should deem chimeras; but we must remember that they had to enter upon an entirely unexplored field, and were at the outset wholly ignorant of even the most simple properties of matter. They were the pioneers in chemistry, and, although often on the wrong track, we must give them credit for faithful and persistent, if not always successful, work.

Amongst those of the Middle Ages who attract most attention for their researches in chemistry are Roger Bacon and Albertus Magnus, both of whom we have already mentioned. The former was undoubtedly acquainted with the composition of gunpowder, although its discovery is usually attributed to another monk of a later date—Schwartz of Cologne. And, strange as it may seem, one that had quite a reputation at this period as an alchemist—the name then used for chemist—was no less a personage than the great philosopher and theologian St. Thomas Aquinas. He not only studied alchemy, but also wrote a work on it entitled *A Treatise on the Essence of Minerals*. He is said to have coined the word amalgam, as it is found for the first time in his work. Philologists, we fancy, would scarcely think of tracing the word to such a source.

Another monk who was in some respects the most remarkable man of his time, and who was certainly the foremost alchemist of his age, was Raymond Lully, a Spanish Franciscan. He was the first to prepare carbonate of potash, essential oils, and to rectify spirits of wine. He likewise introduced an improved method for the cupellation of silver and the preparation of mercury. Later on, Basil Valentine, a German Benedictine, distinguished himself by his many discoveries and by his introduction of qualitative analysis into the study of chemistry. Agricola, born 1490, died 1555, was the first to describe clearly processes of assaying and smelting ores, and for this reason he is considered the founder of that branch of chemistry known as metallurgy. Van Helmont, one of the distinguished alumni of the University of Louvain, was also celebrated for his investigations and for the originality of his work. He was the author of what Louis Figuier declares was "the most important chemical discovery of his age," the discovery of the existence of gases—a word coined by Van Helmont—"the capital fact on which the theories of positive chemistry were at a later period to be based." He and Basil Valentine were among the last of the alchemists of any note, and both of them contributed much to usher in the era of chemistry, as distinguished from that of alchemy.

The late Prof. C. A. Wurtz said that chemistry is a French science. We might go further, and say that it is a Catholic science. Of course we make the same claim for all the sciences, but we think it can be made for chemistry in a special way. Lavoisier of *la belle France* is acknowledged to be the father of modern chemistry. He was the first to introduce the balance in chemical experimentation, and was consequently the originator of quantitative analysis. He also discovered oxygen, although independently made known by two other chemists—Priestly and Scheele—and first made a thorough study of its properties and the part it performs in combustion and respiration. One can name his most important discoveries in a few words, and yet these same discoveries were destined to effect a complete revolution in all the methods and appliances of chemical research. Since Lavoisier's time the French seem to claim chemistry as their science by right of discovery, and as such have made greater advances in its extensive domain than any other people. The Germans have done much, especially in the field of organic chemistry and in the discovery of new elements and compounds; the English and Americans have contributed their quota, at least in certain branches of chemistry; but the working theories of the science, and its philosophy, together with numberless important discoveries bearing on these theories and elucidating the philosophy mentioned, have given to the French a prestige and a position as chemical investigators that place them far in advance of their competitors.

In this case it is unnecessary to mention names to show what the work of the Church has been, as she counts all, or nearly all, who have distinguished themselves by their researches in chemistry as her children. Three of the most distinguished chemists—lately deceased—of modern times were sons of Rome as well as of France. We refer to Henri Victoire Dumas, Michel Chevreul, the celebrated centenarian, and Antoine César Becquerel, creator of the science of electrochemistry. Should we run over the list in other countries, it would still be found that many of the most learned and expert investigators in chemical science follow the teachings of the same faith as their co-laborers in France. But space forbids.

And what about medicine? what about anatomy, physiology, surgery, and clinics? What have Catholics done toward the advancement of these branches of knowledge?

History tells us that they were the foremost in the field, and that they have the first claim on our gratitude for what they have done to ameliorate the ailments and sufferings of poor humanity. For upward of a thousand years priests, as a rule, were physicians of the body as well as of the soul, and for centuries the ablest medical attendants of kings and princes were from the ranks of the clergy.

It was not, however, until the middle of the sixteenth century that anatomy and physiology were put on anything like a scientific basis. Then the work was accomplished by the professors of the great universities of Padua, Pisa, Bologna, and Rome. The most eminent among these professors were Vesalius, Fallopius and Eustachius, Rialdus Columbus, and Fabricius of Aquapendente. The first three named are called by the great naturalist Cuvier "the fathers of modern anatomy." Vesalius was the first to cast aside the *ipse dixit* of Galen, the celebrated Greek physician, whose authority had been regarded as almost supreme for over a thousand years. In spite of the opposition of contemporary physicians, who regarded Galen with the same admiration as philosophers did Aristotle, Vesalius, then only a young man, insisted that the "master," as Galen was called, was wrong in many particulars, and that the time had come for a revision of what was then held regarding anatomy and physiology. Before his time little was known about the human frame or about the functions of its various organs. Though the bones composing the skeleton, the muscles, and some of the nerves had been studied and described, little had been done beyond this. But Vesalius, with the intuition of genius, appealed to nature, and showed, by a study of the human body, that Galen had fallen into many and great errors. The latter had studied human anatomy only analogically, by the dissection of apes and lower animals, whilst Vesalius introduced the method of studying the same science by the dissection of human subjects, and with a result that exceeded his most sanguine expectations.

From this period medicine and the cognate branches made rapid strides onward. And here we would direct attention to an observation of Hallam's, that "the best physicians of the century were either Italian or French." Nay more: in order better to evince how the Church patronized those who had signalized themselves in the study of the branches of which we have been speaking, we would tell how Cesalpino, the forerunner of Harvey in the discovery of the circulation of the blood—some claiming for the former the merit of the actual discovery—was called to Rome by Clement VIII., who made him his physician and appointed him lecturer on medicine in the College of the Sapienza. We would adduce, too, the case of the great naturalist Malpighi, the father of microscopic anatomy and of vegetable physiology. He was the first to apply the microscope in anatomical and physiological inquiries, and with an accuracy and a success that were little short of marvellous. It was he who supplemented the discovery of Harvey regarding the circulation of the blood. Harvey showed experimentally that the blood flowed from the heart through the arteries and returned to the heart through the veins, but he was unable to tell how the blood passed from the arteries to the veins. This Malpighi did by the application of the microscope, when he saw that the transfer was made through those small veins, invisible to unaided vision, called capillaries. In recognition of his eminent merits Innocent XII. called him to Rome and made him his chief physician and chamberlain.

We have referred to Harvey and his discovery of the circulation of the blood. But how much of this discovery was in reality due him? Harvey was a pupil of Fabricius of Aquapendente, a professor in Padua. Fabricius had discovered that the valves of the veins open toward the heart, and consequently that the blood cannot flow back through the veins from the heart. Harvey went one step farther, and showed that the valves of the arteries open from the heart, and therefore that the blood must flow from the heart through the arteries and return to the heart through the veins. Now, observe what was done before him. His master had made the discovery regarding the valves of the veins; Cesalpino had shown the circulation of the blood in the lungs, and, it would seem, understood the nature of the larger circulation also. Harvey supplemented their work by extending what Fabricius had done, and by demonstrating what Cesalpino had stated, but had not proved, regarding the greater circulation. Add to this that it required Malpighi's discovery before the nature of the circulation was fully known, and it will be seen how much the Italians are entitled to what is justly considered one of the greatest discoveries in physiological science. May it not be, after all, that it is the Italian physicians who deserve the credit of the discovery, and that, as has been wittily remarked, Harvey's merit consists in "the circulation of the circulation of the blood" —that is, of publishing it to the world? It would seem so. But no matter. Even on the assumption of Harvey's being the actual discoverer, the glory of the masters is not diminished by the success of their pupil.

Besides the eminent investigators just mentioned, the Church points to others equally renowned. Among these we note the great Morgagni, the founder of pathological anatomy; Spallanzani, the first to trace experimentally the origin of infusoria to atmospheric germs, in opposition to those who maintained the theory of spontaneous generation; the brilliant Bichat, "who instituted and almost originated the study of systematic anatomy." Conspicuous, too, are Paré, the first to introduce a simple and successful treatment of gunshot and other wounds, the same as is now employed; Desault, the originator of clinical and surgical instruction; and the learned Johannes Müller, the reformer of the study of medicine and the founder of the physico-chemical school of physiology, which he raised from a speculative to a positive science. And then we must not forget the eminent French *savant* Claude Bernard, the first to institute a laboratory of physiology—the model of the many biological laboratories now found throughout the world, and the first to apply the experimental method to the study of the functions of nutrition in men and animals, and to promulgate the doctrines now taught regarding these functions.

One more department of knowledge remains to be considered, and then our brief, although, we fear, tedious, review will be at an end. We refer to the natural sciences. The reader is surely prepared, from what we have already said regarding the other sciences, to hear it stated that it was Catholics, too, who were the first to take the initiative in the study of nature. Botany, zoölogy, geology, mineralogy, seem always to have exerted a peculiar fascination over the minds of the children of Holy Church. We may recall the rapturous delight and the impassioned eloquence of a St. Francis of Assisi, of a St. Bernard, or of a Father Faber, when discoursing on the beauties and grandeur of the works of

God as displayed in the natural world. Their sentiments are characteristic in an eminent degree of those which control, more or less, all truly religious minds. In revelation they study God in His word; in nature they study Him in His work. And this study of God in His work has engaged the attention of Christian minds from the earliest times. We have already seen to what an extent it was the case in astronomy and physical science. We have likewise seen how devoted a student of nature was Albert the Great. It is almost superfluous to say that his successors trod in his footsteps. Many of the scholars of the Middle Ages devoted themselves to the study of natural history, as well as to that of philosophy and theology; and with the revival of learning at the period of the *Renaissance* Catholic naturalists were the first to make their influence felt wherever science was cultivated. Italy seems to have contributed most to the early development of the natural sciences, especially of botany and geology. France and Germany are probably entitled to the glory of being the first countries to give a special impetus to the study of zoölogy and mineralogy.

The illustrious Cesalpino, whom we have already mentioned, has always been held in high esteem for his contributions to the science of botany. Cuvier designates his book *De Plantis* as a "work of genius," and he is called by Linnæus, who was indebted to him for his system of classification, "as the first orthodox and systematic botanist." His method is as exact and as logical as that of the best-trained botanist of our own day. "Since all science," says he, "consists in the collection of similar and the distribution of dissimilar things, and since the consequence of this is a distribution into genera and species, which are to be natural classes governed by real differences, I have attempted to execute this task in the whole range of plants." How like is this definition of science by Cesalpino unto that given three hundred years later by one of England's most applauded scientists, Prof. Stanley Jevens, according to whom "science arises from the discovery of identity amidst diversity"!

But although the learned physician of Clement VIII. knew what should be done, he was not able to accomplish the work himself. Still, he laid the foundations so well that he most materially assisted those who were to complete the superstructure. This great work was reserved for Antoine Jussieu, of the famous "botanical dynasty" of France. True, Linnæus had contributed toward the advance of the science of botany by his *Artificial System*, which so much simplified its study, but no one knew better than he its defects. During his whole life he worked at the natural system pointed out by Cesalpino, and declared it to be the "first and last desideratum" toward placing botany on a scientific basis. Bernard Jussieu tackled the problem in the arrangement of the plants of the garden of the Trianon, but died, leaving his method unpublished. This, however, was accomplished by his nephew Antoine, who gave to the world, and in a wonderfully developed state, the first natural system, described in his *General Plantarum.* Of this work, which appeared in 1789, Cuvier remarked that it "forms perhaps as important an epoch in the science of observation as the *Chemistry* of Lavoisier does in the sciences of experiment."

As in geography, so in botany, a great deal of our knowledge is due to Catholic missionaries, especially those of the various religious orders. While laboring for the salvation of souls these learned men were not oblivious of the beauties of the vegetable world with which they everywhere came in contact. Father F. Lopez de Gomara was the first to make known the remarkable flora of Mexico. Father C. Plumier, of the order of Minims, by order of Louis XIV., visited America and the West India Islands in the interests of botany. An idea of the magnitude of his work may be inferred from the fact that he designed over six thousand figures of American plants, and that a part of his manuscripts, preserved in the Museum of Paris, forms twenty-two volumes in folio. Father Louis Feuillée, of the same order and about the same time, published his history of medicinal plants of Peru and Chili. Father Michel Boym, a Polish Jesuit, published in 1659 the first outline of the flora of China. Father Charlevoix, S. J., made known the plants of Canada, whilst his *confrères*, Fathers Acosta, Kamel, Gui Tachard, De Beze, and De Loureiro, did the same respectively for the flora of the Indies, the Philippine Islands, Siam, Malacca, and Cochin China.

And here let us indicate the origin of the name of those beautiful flowers that every one so much admires—we mean camellias. Did it ever occur to any of our readers that they take their name from that of a Jesuit priest? And yet it is so. They were introduced into Europe by the Father Kamel just named, and the great botanist Linnæus gracefully called them camellias—a name they have since borne. This is one of many similar instances that might be cited. Those familiar with the history and nomenclature of botany will readily recall others.

In speaking of chemistry we had occasion to refer to Agricola and what he accomplished for mineralogy and mining. The one, however, who did most to advance the science of mineralogy, and the one to create the science of crystallography as it is now studied, was René Just Haüy, professor of the Institute of France, and a man of such renown that Lavoisier, Berthollet, La Place, Lagrange, and others of the ablest scientists of

France attended his lectures. But who was Haüy? A humble French priest and a canon of the Cathedral of Notre Dame in Paris.

In his *History of Civilization in England*, speaking of Haüy, Mr. Buckle says: "This remarkable man achieved a complete union between mineralogy and geometry, and, bringing the laws of space to bear on the molecular arrangements of matter, was able to penetrate into the intimate structure of crystals." Continuing the same subject, he observes: "To ascertain that violations of symmetry are susceptible of mathematical calculation was to make a vast addition to our knowledge; but what seems to me still more important is that it indicates an approach to the magnificent idea that everything which occurs is regulated by law, and that confusion and disorder are impossible."

Geology, like botany, found, as we have remarked, its cradle in Italy; and to the same country it owes nearly all of its early development. The first to entertain sound views regarding geological phenomena was the famous artist Leonardo da Vinci, who died in 1519. Hallam regards Da Vinci as occupying the foremost rank among the illustrious men of the fifteenth century, and considers "his anticipations of the great discoveries in astronomy, geology, and other sciences as almost preternatural." He was succeeded by Fracastoro, Vallisneri, Scilla, Moro; Generelli, a Carmelite friar; Steno, Danish bishop of Heliopolis, *in partibus infidelium*, who spent a great part of his life in Italy; and Spada, a priest of Grezzana. To these earnest students of Nature belongs the glory of laying, almost alone, the foundations of the science of geology. In the introduction to his admirable *Principles of Geology*, Sir Charles Lyell says, in referring to the work of these investigators: "I return with pleasure to the geologists of Italy, who preceded, as has already been shown, the naturalists of other countries in their investigations into the ancient history of the earth, and who still maintained a decided pre-eminence. They refuted and ridiculed the physico-theological systems of Burnet, Whiston, and Woodward; while Vallisneri, in his commentary on the Woodwardian theory, remarked how much the interests of religion, as well as those of sound philosophy, had suffered by perpetually mixing up the sacred writings with questions in physical science." In speaking of Vallisneri, he says: "The works of this author were rich in original observations. He attempted the first general sketch of the marine deposits of Italy, their geographical extent, and most characteristic organic remains." In a word, Vallisneri was the first to make anything approaching a geological survey. The same learned author pronounces Friar Generelli's work "an admirable essay," and considers that of Bishop Steno, published in 1669, as "the most remarkable of the period."

It would take too long to tell how perfectly the children of the Church continued the work which they began so well. Suffice it to say that they have never allowed their interest in geological investigation to relax, and that some of the ablest work accomplished by contemporary geologists is to be credited to ecclesiastics. In evidence of the truth of this statement we need only mention among many the names of the Abbés Delaunay, Bourgeois, Renard, Ducrost, Arcelin, Béroud, Cau Durban, Hamard of the Oratory, and Mgr. Castracane of Rome—all known as occupying positions in the front rank of European geologists and prehistoric archæologists.

After what we have said of the various natural sciences, it is scarcely necessary to delay on the subject of zoölogy. The earliest and most successful cultivators of this science—taking it up pretty much as old Aristotle had left it—were the Italians and French. Aldrovandus's *Storia Naturale*, in thirteen volumes, published in the latter part of the sixteenth century, and the great *Histoire Naturelle* of Buffon and Daubenton, must ever be regarded of such importance toward the development of zoölogy as to entitle their authors to be ranked with Aristotle as founders of the science.

So much for the different sciences which we

have been considering. But the Church has contributed to the advancement of science in many other ways besides those already mentioned. We have named some eminent scientists, among them Galileo, who were pensioners of the Pope, but it is a matter of history that there have been as many as fifty or more at a time who were granted annuities by the Roman Pontiffs, both as a reward for their labors and that they might the more easily continue their researches.

Besides, the means of successfully studying science were first afforded where the influence of the Church was most felt—we mean in Italy. She was celebrated not only for her universities—of which she possessed a greater number than any other country, and of such reputation that students flocked to them from all parts of Europe—but also as being the first country to establish museums of natural history, botanic gardens, and to organize scientific societies—the forerunners of those learned scientific bodies which are now found in every civilized country.

The first museum of any consequence, and noted at the time for the number and variety of its minerals and fossils, was that of the Vatican in Rome. There were others in the various universities of Italy, but their establishment was of a subsequent date. Those of other countries came afterward.

The first botanical garden established in Europe

was that of Pisa, in 1543. The next was instituted in Padua in 1545; then the one in Florence in 1556; and that of Bologna in 1568. That of the Vatican dates from the same year. The first established north of the Alps came several years later, whilst those of Upsala, Amsterdam, and Oxford were not thought of until the last quarter of the seventeenth century.

The first scientific society was that founded by Porta in Naples in 1560, and called Academia dei Segreti. The Academia dei Lincei followed in Rome in 1609. The celebrated Academia del Cimento was founded in Florence in 1657, and ten years later it published its first collection of experiments—a publication that served as a model of the reports published subsequently by similar societies.

But our task, although drawing to an end, is not yet finished. During the course of this chapter we have referred incidentally to some of the discoveries and inventions of Catholic scientists, but we have not told all. Neither have we told of the introduction of many important industries which have materially contributed, directly or indirectly, to the advancement of science. It would require a volume even to outline what Catholics have done in this respect; but there are a few inventions and industries to which we must direct attention, notwithstanding the limited space at our disposal. In this age of distorted history one is apt to ignore what the Church and her sons have done, and to forget that it is to them that we are indebted for nearly everything—we might say everything—that we now regard as essential to the comforts and luxuries of our boasted modern civilization.

We have spoken of the invention of the telescope and microscope in Catholic Italy, and of the grand revolution effected in science consequent on their application. The most important invention, however, and the one that aided most in the diffusion of knowledge, was that of printing, due to Gutenberg, in 1436. This invention—which, in the hands of Gutenberg and his co-laborers Faust and Schœffer, was the marvel of the world at the time, on account of the rapidity and perfection with which books were multiplied by its means—anticipated by nearly a century the much-lauded reformation of Luther. And all necessary preparations had been made for this glorious invention. Cotton paper was ready, and had been used in Italy since the tenth century; and linen paper, according to Hallam, was invented in the century following. The first newspaper was published in Venice in 1562.

The first printing-press introduced into England was set up by Caxton in 1477 in Westminster Abbey. The then ruling abbot, John Estney, read the first proof of the first English translation of the Bible ever printed in Great Britain, and the first printer lived and died in the Abbey.

The first printing-press used in America was brought from Spain, about 1540, by the first bishop and archbishop of Mexico, the zealous and enlightened Don Fray Juan Zumarraga. "The first viceroy of New Spain, Mendoza," we quote from the learned Bishop Montez de Oca, "helped the archbishop in his glorious work; the celebrated editor Cromberger of Seville furnished the materials and the men; John Pablos was the name of the typographer chosen to cross the Atlantic; and an abridgment of Christian doctrine, in both the Spanish and Aztec languages, was the first book ever issued by the press in the New World."

Clocks may be looked upon as the joint production of three monks, as each had more or less to do with their construction. These monks were the illustrious Gerbert, Pacifico of Verona, and Abbot William of Hirschau, Germany. Watches were invented as early as the fifteenth century, since Nuremberg was celebrated for those manufactured there about the third quarter of the century. Spectacles were first constructed by Salvino, an Italian monk, in 1285. Some years before, Roger Bacon, in referring to a plano-convex lens, had spoken of the benefit of it to old men and "to those who have weak eyes" in reading and viewing small objects.

Schwartz, a monk of Cologne, first prepared gunpowder about 1320. Fire-arms were introduced before the end of the century. The thermometer was invented by Santorio of Italy, early in the seventeenth century. A few years afterward the mercurial barometer was invented by a countryman of his, Evangelista Torricelli. The camera-obscura, that all-important instrument in photography, was invented some time during the sixteenth century by the founder of the first scientific society, Giambattista della Porta. The first photographs were taken in 1839 by two Frenchmen—Niepce and Daguerre. The magic lantern, an instrument that has of late years proved of such value in the hands of scientists and educators, was the invention of the learned Jesuit Father Kircher, who died in 1680.

Flavio di Gioja invented the mariner's compass early in the fourteenth century. But the navigator needed something more, and this something was furnished him in 1569 by a pupil of the University of Louvain, Gerard Mercator, the inventor of the chart that bears his name. "Such is the suitableness," it has been said, " of Mercator's projection to the use of the mariner's compass that the latter seems to have been an incomplete discovery until the announcement of the former." The Portuguese were the first to use the astrolabe in navigation; and the celebrated mathematician Pedro Nunez, in his book on vavigation, published in 1537, was the first to direct special attention to the quadrant, now replaced by the sextant as a substitute for the astrolabe and other instruments for observation that had previously been used. The log, according to Humboldt, was in use before this period. It is mentioned by Friar Pigafetta, the historiographer of Magellan's voyage around the globe, as a well-known means of measuring the distance made by a vessel at sea.

Locks for canals are of Italian origin. Watermills and water-engines were invented by Leonardo da Vinci. Terrestrial and celestial globes were first used for illustrating lectures by the famous Gerbert; and—would it be credited?—he was the first to construct a steam-organ, something that has been dubbed as a recent American invention, under the name of "calliope."

The apparatus—now so common—for the generation of the electric light, and known as dynamo-electric machines, are frequently pointed to as examples of American skill and invention; but nothing could be further from the truth. Nollet and Van Malderan of Belgium, about thirty years ago, constructed the first magneto-electric machine for producing the electric light—a type of machine still in use. In 1860, Dr. Antonio Pacinotti, a professor in Florence, devised an electro-magnetic machine which embodied in principle all that we find in the more improved dynamos of to-day. Pacinotti's great invention was the armature he employed, of which all the armatures now in use are only modifications. A few years later the subject was taken up by M. Gramme, a Belgian mechanic, and his experiments resulted in 1871, in the production of the first successful modern type of dynamo that was put on the market.

M. Gramme is likewise the inventor of the electro-motor, as he was the first to discover the reversibility of the armature of a dynamo on the passage through it of an electric current. This was justly pronounced by the eminent English physicist Prof. Clerke Maxwell the greatest discovery of the present half the nineteenth century.

The first electric lamp was invented by Leon Faucault in 1848. The carbons used for electric lights are the invention of M. Carré. The first storage battery, than which nothing seems to promise greater or more important results in the near future, is due to Gaston Planté, a member of the Catholic Scientific Society of Brussels.

Benjamin Franklin is reputed to be the discoverer of the identity of electricity and lightning, and of the issuing of electricity from metallic points; but the credit of both these discoveries must be given to a Bohemian monk, Procopius Diwisch. He was also the inventor of the first lightning-rod. And while this poor and forgotten priest was making his great discoveries "Franklin was receiving his first lessons in electricity from Dr. Spence."

So it is in regard to the steam-engine. Watt is usually considered its inventor; and yet patents were taken out for steam-engines—and practical working engines, too—a full century before Watt commenced his experiments on the Newcomen engine. And this engine, to which Watt did no more than to make some additions, was, after all, only an improvement on an engine constructed by Savery, who appropriated *in toto* the work and inventions of the Marquis of Worcester. And this Marquis of Worcester, the first inventor of an actual steam-engine, for which he received a patent from Parliament in 1663—just one hundred years before Watt took up a model of a Newcomen engine in Glasgow College, and one hundred and nine years before he took out his first patent—was a devout Catholic.

So, too, is it respecting the application of steam to propelling boats. Robert Fulton is famed as the inventor of the steamboat; and still he was not its inventor. Far back in 1543, Blasco de Garay, a Spanish sea-captain, exhibited in the harbor of Barcelona, in presence of Charles V. and many of his court, a boat propelled by steam, which was capable of going at the rate of a league an hour. Blasco de Garay's invention lay dormant for more than two centuries. Toward the latter part of the eighteenth century the subject was taken up again by several persons in Europe and in this country, and eventually resulted in Robert Fulton's *Clermont*, which made her trial trip from New York to Albany in January, 1808.

The manufacture and application of illuminating gas is usually regarded as an English *invention*. In 1792, Wm. Murdock used coal-gas to light his workshops at Redruth in Cornwall. But it is a matter of record that eight years before, Jean Pierre Minkelers, a professor in the University of Louvain, had made use of the same gas to light his lecture-rooms. To this same professor is also due the first application of coal-gas to balloons—the invention of two Frenchmen, Stephen and Joseph Montgolfier—although the credit of it is usually given to the English aëronaut Green.

Let these examples suffice for the present. We might add to the list, and show also how the inventions themselves have been improved and perfected. But this would not strengthen the proposition we wish to prove—viz. that Catholics were always originators and pioneers in every branch of invention and discovery. Others may contribute toward the development of what Catholics have begun, but *facile est addere inventis*—"it is easy to add to inventions."

We insist on this point, as it is specially important. "The invention of an instrument," says Stanley Jevons, "has usually marked, if it has not made, an epoch. The science of heat might be said to commence with the construction of the thermometer, and it has been recently advanced by the construction of the thermo-electric pile. Chemistry has been created chiefly by the careful use of the balance, which forms a unique instance of an instrument remaining substantially in the form in which it was first applied to scientific purposes by Archimedes. The balance never has been, and probably never can be, improved except in details of construction. The torsion balance, introduced by Coulomb toward the end of the last century, has rapidly become essential in many branches of investigation. In the hands of Cavendish and Bailey it gave a determination of the earth's density; applied to the galvanometer, it gave a delicate measure of electrical forces; and it is indispensable in the thermo-electric pile."

And there are yet a few more contributions of a different kind that we can not pass over in silence.

They do not bear directly on the advance of science, but they illustrate so well what we have been speaking of—viz. that we owe so much of what conduces to our comfort and well-being to Catholic sources—that they deserve a mention.

We all love music. It was the monk Guido of Arezzo who invented the gamut, in 1124. He was also the inventor of the cymbals and the heptachord, the precursor of the piano and other stringed instruments of a later date. Organs were invented in Italy in the eighth century. Church-bells were introduced by St. Paulinus, bishop of Nola, in Campania, about A. D. 400, whence the name *nola* or *campana*—bell—still retained in several European languages.

The first bank was founded in 1171, in Venice. Letters of exchange were introduced in Barcelona early in the fifteenth century. Book-keeping is of Italian origin, and the first treatise on the subject was written by the author of the first work on algebra, the monk Luca Paccioli, and published in Venice in 1495. Post-offices were established in France and Italy early in the twelfth century. The stone-coal industry was first developed in England about the middle of the ninth century, and by monks. Glass windows were introduced in the third and fourth centuries, and stained glass during the Middle Ages.

Cotton-culture was introduced into Spain in the tenth century, and was extended to Sicily and Italy shortly after. The silkworm was unknown in Europe before the reign of Justinian, when it was brought from the East to Constantinople by two monks. Tea was first imported by the Portuguese in the beginning of the sixteenth century. Coffee was brought to Venice about a century later. Quinine was made known in Europe by the Jesuit missionaries, and from this circumstance it was named Jesuits' bark. To the missionaries we are also indebted for the knowledge of many other plants used in medicine and the arts.

Sir Walter Raleigh is usually credited with introducing the potato into Europe from Virginia; and yet there is the best of evidence to show that it was brought to Spain from Quito at a much earlier period. In 1588, two years after Raleigh is said to have carried it to England, it was sent to Flanders from Italy, where it had been received from Spain, in which country it had been cultivated as an article of food for many years. Indeed, the same year, 1586, in which the English navigator is said to have taken the potato to his country, it was described by the botanist Charles de l'Ecluse as being well known and commonly used.

Knives and forks and wheelbarrows, like so many other common but useful things, are of Italian origin. The hydraulic press was invented by Pascal. Artesian wells were first used in Modena, and were made known in France by the astronomer Cassini, where they were given the name they now bear. The one to regulate the clock of time by the calendar we now use was Pope Gregory XIII., aided by the Catholic astronomers of Europe.

And so we might continue the list almost indefinitely. But it is not our purpose to give the history of science, and so we arrest ourselves here. We should like to tell what the Church and her children have done toward the development of the sciences and inventions of which they are, as it were, joint authors; we should love, too, to tell more of the labors of the Catholic scientists of England, Germany, Belgium, America, and other parts of the world, especially in more recent times and in our own day; but we can not do so now. We have barely alluded to a few of them, but we are satisfied to let the reader judge of their present work by what they have accomplished in the past. *Ab uno disce omnes.*

That great statesman and scholar W. E. Gladstone expresses in one sentence all that might be said on the subject when he declares that "since the first three hundred years of persecution the Roman Catholic Church has marched for fifteen hundred years at the head of human civilization, and has driven, harnessed to its chariot as the horses of a triumphal car, the chief intellectual and material forces of the world; its art, the art of the world; its genius, the genius of the world; its greatness, glory, grandeur, and majesty have been almost, though not absolutely, all that, in these respects, the world has had to boast of."

In our introduction we asked our readers to consider not only what the Church has done directly, through her sons, but also what she has accomplished indirectly, by her influence. After all we have said it is unnecessary for us to dwell on this point at length. We prefer to let our readers draw their own conclusions. The influence of an organization that has always been so active, always foremost in the march of progress, can have been in but one direction—forward, *excelsior*. We may look back on the Church at any period of her history, and we shall find that she was progressive then as she is to-day; that then, as now, she was the one power capable of directing and carrying with her the genius of the world.

Judging her children, who have reflected such honor on her, we repeat, with Lord Macaulay: "The question with respect to them is not where they were, but which way they were going. Were their faces set in the right or wrong direction? Were they in the front or rear of their generation? Did they exert themselves to help onward the great movement of the human race, or to stop it? This is not charity, but simple justice and common sense. It is the fundamental law of the world in which we live that truth shall grow—first the blade, then the ear, after that the full corn in the ear." Judged by this standard in her relation to the advancement of science, the Church, as represented by her children, is all that we have claimed she has been, and still is—the sole possessor of the sceptre of Science in the whole of Christendom.

CHAPTER III.

CATHOLIC DOGMA AND SCIENTIFIC DOGMATISM.

IT is now about a third of a century since the attention of the world was specially directed to the theory of man's natural origin by the process of organic evolution. Since then all kinds of surmises and speculations, with a certain school whose principles are naturally opposed to those of the Church, have passed current as science, and have been pointed to as indisputable evidence of the advance of modern thought. Because the Church has not endorsed the opinions that have so universally obtained outside her pale, she has been decried as the enemy of progress and enlightenment. Because her children have scrupulously eschewed all theories that conflicted with the teachings of their faith, they have been stigmatized as inimical to science, and accused of retarding its advancement. In a word, it has been proclaimed that the Church has now, and always has had, a baneful influence on science and on those who would devote themselves to scientific research, and that, consequently, science and her votaries have nothing of good to expect from the

Church, or from those who acknowledge adhesion to her authority, and who subscribe unreservedly to her doctrines.

The subject-matter, then, of these charges—the influence of the Church on the progress of science—will bear more than a cursory examination. And in order that the results of this influence may be brought out in a brighter light—an influence that bears to the doctrines of the Church almost the same relation that effect does to cause—we shall contrast it with the influences that are non-Catholic and anti-Catholic.

That there may be no misunderstanding about the use of terms employed during the course of this chapter, it may at once be premised that, unless otherwise specified, the general term "science" will be used to designate what are ordinarily known as the natural and physical sciences—those sciences, namely, that are based on observation and experiment, and whose various data are co-ordinated by induction.

We shall, in the first place, briefly define the relation between religion and experimental science, and then refer in a few words to the dependence of the various empirical sciences on philosophy—the science of principles. After this we shall inquire who are popularly reckoned as the chief representatives and exponents of what is known as modern science. We shall next give a brief account of what these alleged masters of science are supposed to have accomplished, and what contributions they are reputed to have made to the general stock of human knowledge. We shall then compare the conclusions of various investigators of recognized authority, and ask our readers, on the evidence presented, to form their own opinions of what we are constantly called upon to accept as science in its latest and most advanced phase.

In contemplating the relation between religion and science, between dogma and the results arrived at by experiment and induction, the first thing that must arrest one's attention is the responsibility that attaches to any body or organization that claims authority to teach in matters of religion. When an individual or an organization claims to have received a divine commission to teach and preach, there is immediately and necessarily associated with such a commission an idea of infallibility that cannot be separated from the commission any more than it can be separated from truth itself.

For this reason all religious bodies, as well as their founders, are responsible not only for the errors they teach directly, but also for those which they teach by implication. For this reason, too, they are accountable for errors in matters of science and philosophy when such errors are logically deducible from doctrines that are considered as a part of the creed proclaimed or of the faith professed. And yet more: in addition to the errors that they directly or indirectly teach as organized bodies, they are likewise amenable for the errors of individuals affiliated to them whenever such errors are the logical outgrowth from principles generally maintained, or from tenets accepted, by the bodies in question, as fundamental. The truth of this view is so plain that it cannot be gainsaid. It is based on simple common sense, and no one endowed with ordinary reasoning capacity would have the hardihood to contradict it any more than he would call in question a self-evident truth of philosophy or mathematics.

Of all the religious organizations, however, that ask us to give our assent to their teachings, there is only one that is equal to such a responsibility, only one that can meet such exacting requirements as those just enumerated; and that body is the Catholic Church. It alone, of all religious denominations, has taught, and it alone can teach, the truths of faith without in any way or in any instance contradicting the certain declarations of science, and without in the slightest degree impeding its development. It alone, in virtue of the truths embodied in its doctrines, aids and fosters science, and, by reason of the light which it sheds, prevents the student of science from going astray, when, if deprived of such light, a lapse into the most pernicious errors would often be almost, if not quite, inevitable.

The Church, it is true, has no mission to teach science. Her mission is to save souls. Neither has she any "call to watch over and protect science." Nevertheless, owing to the intimate connection between revelation and nature, the truths of theology cannot entirely be separated from those of science without great detriment to the latter. For this reason Cardinal Newman, in his admirable *Idea of a University*, justly observes that "a university cannot exist externally to the Catholic pale, for it cannot teach universal knowledge if it does not teach Catholic theology." For the same reason he declares that "to withdraw theology from the public schools is to impair the completeness and invalidate the trustworthiness of all that is actually taught in them." For a similar reason, also, he asserts that "revealed truth enters to a very great extent into the province of science, philosophy, and literature, and to put it on one side in compliment to secular science is simply under color of a compliment to do science a great damage." Scientists, then, require the guidance of other truths than those deduced from observation and experiment. They must have recourse to another and higher order of knowledge—to revelation—to be able to draw just conclusions even in their own special spheres of research. Without the light of revealed truth "they say what is true *exceptis excipiendis;* what is true, but what requires guarding; true, but must not be ridden too hard or made what is called a *hobby;* true, but not the measure of all things; true, but, if thus inordinately, extravagantly, ruinously carried out, in spite of other sciences, in spite of theology, sure to become but a great bubble, and burst."

It is important to bear these facts in mind when we consider the weight of responsibility resting on the various religious sects, scattered throughout the world, for the errors of their individual members. The fact that a member of any sect, in following out to its logical consequences any principle or doctrine, may go farther than do the authors or recognized leaders of such sect, does not remove the responsibility from the sect to the individual. The individual is logical, consistent; the sect and its authors and promoters are not; and these latter, therefore, must bear the responsibility of all errors evolved from the doctrines taught, when such doctrines come within the scope of the creed professed.

Thus Mohammedanism is answerable for the errors of those who accept its teachings, in so far as such errors proceed from or are the natural outgrowth of Mohammedan doctrines or principles. The Koran, for instance, distinctly proclaims the Ptolemaic theory of the universe, and to this theory every good Mussulman is committed. The Hindoo religion also teaches a false system of astronomy, and likewise false systems of anatomy and physiology. These systems every devout Hindoo must accept as so many articles of faith, inasmuch as his faith is so interwoven with false, scientific systems that it is inseparable from them. Swedenborgianism labors under the same difficulty. The revelations of its founder, aside from objections that may be urged against them on other grounds, are discredited by his erroneous statements regarding the planets and solar system.

In the instances just quoted we have spoken of religious organizations and their founders as directly and explicitly teaching what is demonstrably false in science. But there are other and more numerous and more serious cases, wherein scientific errors are engendered and fostered indirectly. It may be on account of adopting some false principle of philosophy or theology, and making it the basis of a system of belief. The extent of the application of the principle asserted may not be perceived by the originator of the system, but when it is carried by others to its logical consequences, it is found to be fraught with disaster and ruin.

Luther's principle of private interpretation of the Bible is a case in point. Its logical sequence is rationalism and infidelity; and rationalism and infidelity have given birth not only to the materialism, pantheism, agnosticism, and atheism which prevail to such an alarming extent in our day, but also to all those false and absurd theories in philosophy and science that have been so rife during the last three and a half centuries.

Luther's principle, however, is only one among many that have equally impeded the progress of true science. The rejection of authority, the denial of the existence and necessity of revelation, the assertion of the sufficiency of human reason for the discussion and solution of all problems in philosophy, seem at first sight to have little connection with the progress of natural and physical science; and yet, as Cardinal Newman has demonstrated in the masterly work above quoted, nothing could be more prejudicial to them, or oppose greater barriers against their development.

Examine we now the principles of the various bodies that are opposed to the Catholic Church, and consider the doctrines of the different denominations that have protested against her authority, rejected her teaching, and discarded her philosophy no less than her theology, and we shall see how wide-reaching is the blighting influence already alluded to, and how much of the error in every department of knowledge these same organizations can be indicted for, and that, too, by reason of the principles they maintain and the doctrines they inculcate.

One of the great glories of the Church is the introduction by her children of the experimental or inductive method into the study of natural and physical science. It was by studying nature in accordance with the principles of induction that the great Catholic scientists from Galileo and Pascal to our own time have been so successful in their investigations, and have been able to do so much genuine work in all the branches of science. But, while recognizing the value of the inductive philosophy as an aid to the study of nature, and to co-ordinating the countless facts and phenomena which came before them, these illustrious sons of Holy Church knew well the extent of its availability as an instrument of research. They were ever conscious that the sphere of its application was circumscribed, and was limited to the discussion of facts and phenomena fully observed and classified, and to conclusions legitimately drawn from such facts and phenomena. They recognized all along the existence of higher and more trustworthy guides—a Christian metaphysics and a divine revelation—to which their inductive philosophy was always made subservient. Over and above their knowledge of facts and their inductions therefrom, they ever retained a science of principles which, corroborated and supplemented by the truths of revelation, prevented them from falling into error.

But see how different it is with those who ignore the principles of metaphysics, and who reject the teachings of revelation. Instead of taking the inductive method for what it really is—one of the branches of philosophy to be confined within the domain of the empirical branches—they employ it to the exclusion of all other aids and methods. In a word, they deny revelation, and relegate philosophy as a science of principles to the unknown and unknowable. This is what has been done, and what is being done, by a constantly increasing number of men who call themselves scientists and "advanced thinkers."

Take Herbert Spencer, for instance. He is looked upon as one of the leading philosophers of the day, and has a large following of enthusiastic admirers. But his *New Philosophy*, in spite of all representations to the contrary, teaches, either directly or by implication, the rankest materialism and the most downright atheism. He, however, is simply carrying out the infidel and rationalistic principles of the reformers of the sixteenth century, and as such may justly be regarded as a scientific exponent of their principles and as an advanced disciple of their irreligious teachings. The same may be said of many of his contemporaries who are regarded as occupying a front rank among modern scientists.

Tyndall, Huxley, Darwin, Hæckel, Vogt, Büchner, Moleschott, Paul Bert, and others of that ilk belong to the same school, as their principles—if principles they can be said to have—are essentially the same. Denying the knowability of God, cause, creation, being, substance, they have left only phenomena; and, rejecting revelation and philosophy as a science of principles, there remains to them only the experimental or inductive method of arriving at truth. They sin by adopting as the only source of knowledge a method that was employed by Catholic scientists in the study of the physical sciences only, and then as subservient always to a higher philosophy. They abuse a system which is good, indeed, in its proper sphere, but which is worthless outside of that sphere, or when taken as a substitute for metaphysics.

Others there are who still give metaphysics a place in their sciences, but who fail to distinguish properly between the functions of metaphysical principles and the office of simple induction. They confound the former with the latter, and give to induction powers it does not and cannot possess. They do not, it is true, like those of whom we have just been speaking, use it as the sole method of philosophy, but give it a prominence which it cannot hold and for which it was never intended. One class sins by exclusiveness—by accepting only the empirical method, rejecting metaphysics entirely; the other, by giving it an exaggerated importance, and allowing philosophy as a science of principles only a secondary place, when by its very nature it should occupy the first.

But what, it may be asked, have false principles

of philosophy or theology to do with the advance of experimental science? How can the religious systems of the reformers of the sixteenth century be construed to be an obstacle, direct or indirect, to progress in geology, zoölogy, astronomy, or any other of the natural sciences? We need not go far for an answer. They impede the proper development of science and retard its progress by giving us false views of nature, and by preventing us from looking upon nature in its entirety and as related to God its Author. These false systems throw men into the babit of speculating, and of evolving theories and imagining them to be so much positive knowledge. They lead men to take hypotheses for demonstration, to accept the opinions and guesses of individuals for genuine science. In a word, they make the followers of these systems spend their time in weaving from the webs of their inner consciousness idle fancies, instead of contributing by genuine work to the advance of practical science and true philosophy.

Let us illustrate. Among the modern scientists who are best known and who have been most applauded are Tyndall, Huxley, Charles Darwin, and Ernst Hæckel, "the Darwin of Germany." But who are these men, and on what does their reputation rest? Popular scientific speculators, known solely by their extravagant and materialistic theories. "Advanced thinkers," forsooth, who have gained an ephemeral notoriety by dressing up in modern scientific terminology the oft-rehashed theories of Leucippus, Heraclitus, and Epicurus. Separate their theories from their contributions to real science, and what is left? What have they done for the advance of science to gain the gratitude of their fellows? Let us see.

Tyndall was for many years lecturer on natural philosophy in the Royal Institution of Great Britain, and was in this capacity the successor of the illustrious Faraday and the great Sir Humphrey Davy. But what a pigmy by the side of these eminent students of nature! Tyndall has been a popular lecturer, it is true, and a clever experimenter, and, with many, a fascinating theorizer, but we do not think one can say more of him. He has done some little original work in physics, in lines pointed out by others, but there is nothing in the intellectual make-up of the man to entitle him to be considered a deep thinker, and nothing has he done by invention or discovery in the realm of nature to justify one in putting him above a second-rate or third-rate scientist. One can find dozens among his contemporaries, who, although less known to the general public, stand head and shoulders above him in his special branches of research. As a physicist and as a mathematician the late Professor Clerk Maxwell was a giant compared with Tyndall, and yet the notoriety of the latter, with those who know no better, is considered as proof of his intellectual superiority over the former. What has been said of Maxwell can with equal truth be said of the eminent physicist Sir William Thompson, P. G. Tait, Gabriel Stokes, Sir G. B. Airy, late Astronomer Royal, and many others of his countrymen, who, although less known to the public than Tyndall, are considered by those who are cognizant of their relative abilities, and of what they have severally done for science, as deserving to be classed with a different caste.

Professor Tyndall has published some interesting lectures and notes of lectures on sound, heat, light, and electricity, and some original memoirs on the same subjects, the latter of which are known only to a limited number of specialists in science; but we venture to assert that he owes more of his celebrity—if we should not rather call it notoriety—to some of his speculative discourses than to all his other writings taken together. Prominent among such discourses we would mention two: that on *The Scientific Use of the Imagination*, and his address before the British Association for the Advancement of Science, at Belfast. In the latter particularly he tries, like many of his co-workers, to apply the experimental method—the only one with which he has any acquaintance—to the discussion of the profoundest questions of philosophy and religion, to both of which, by the way, he is an utter stranger. Here he lays aside the mask which had before so ill concealed the irreligious tendencies of his teachings, and boldly proclaims the baldest materialism, declaring that he sees in matter "the promise and potency of all terrestrial life."

Huxley is celebrated in Europe and in this country as one of the foremost representatives of modern thought. He has held in various institutions of Great Britain the position of professor of biology and comparative anatomy, and has, when confining himself within his proper sphere and to methods with which he is familiar, done much for which he deserves well of science. As a skilful investigator in some departments of natural science he has won for himself an enviable position among contemporary scientists. But how many know Huxley for the real, practical work which he has accomplished? How many have ever heard of his actual contributions to science? How many, even among those who talk so glibly about his views, can give even a partial list of the facts and phenomena to which he first directed attention? Not one in a thousand; not one in ten thousand. They know that he is an exponent of evolution, and that, for some reason or other, he ranks high among modern agnostics, and that he maintains that animals are only conscious automata. They may know, too, that he holds that protoplasm is the physical basis of life, and that he finds an argument for evolution in the bones of the fore-legs of the horse, as studied in the light of certain fossils recently discovered in our western prairies; but, as a rule, their knowledge respecting him and his teachings goes no further. Like Tyndall, Huxley is celebrated as a popular lecturer, and as the author of several volumes of addresses, lectures, and reviews in which he makes known his views on nature, matter, force, life, and which, like Tyndall's views, imply, if they do not always express, the most pronounced forms of materialism and pantheism.

What has been said of Tyndall and Huxley can, in great measure, be repeated respecting Darwin. As a close, patient, intelligent observer of facts and phenomena in the various forms of animal and vegetable life he has had few if any superiors. No one who reads his works can help admiring the ingenuity and the fertility of resource which he displays in his investigations, and the various devices which he makes use of in attaining to a knowledge of the laws and processes of nature, as displayed in the animal and vegetable worlds. But here his merit ends. The conclusions he draws from the facts he has so diligently studied, the theories he bases on them, would be discreditable to the veriest tyro in logic. And what impresses one painfully in reading the works of Darwin, and of those belonging to his school, is the thought—we should say fact—that he is all along directing all his energies not so much to increase our knowledge of nature as to establish and corroborate a pet theory. All his observations and experiments are made with that end in view, and they are often marshalled together irrespective of their real bearing on the theory in question. Facts are presented, assumptions made, and conclusions drawn with a recklessness and a disregard of the simplest rules of dialectics that are simply amazing. Did one not know how often "the wish is father to the thought," and to what an extent a passionate adherence to preconceived notions can render one oblivious to the simplest principles of reasoning, one should find the feebleness of his attempts at argumentation simly unexplainable. In the case of Darwin, however, these glaring defects of logic and his striking lack of consistency are frequently passed over by the average reader unnoticed. The interest excited by the facts presented by the author, the charm of his style, and the fascinating manner in which he groups together the facts and phenomena of which he treats captivate the mind to such an extent that one loses sight of the connection between the premises laid down and the conclusions drawn from them.

And even in his speculations, what has Darwin done but revamp, in such a way as to embrace a larger number of facts and phenomena, a theory that has been maintained, under one form or another, ever since the time of the earliest philosophers of ancient Greece? Darwin's theory of development, or evolution by "natural selection" and "the survival of the fittest," is only a modern way of putting the hypotheses of Anaximander, Empedocles, Heraclitus, Anaxagoras, Democritus, Aristotle, Epicurus, and Lucretius among the ancients, and those of Kant, Oken, Lamarck, and others among the moderns. The author of *The Descent of Man* and *The Origin of Species*, far from originality, has not even the merit of novelty. He simply brings together and collates the observations of others, and, adding them to his own, gives forth to a sensation-loving world an old theory decked out in a garment of many colors, and cut according to the requirements of the prevailing fashion of that capricious modiste ycleped "Modern Science."

And this is what Darwin has contributed to the general treasury of natural knowledge. He wrote many books and spent a long life in the fruitless work of presenting in a new form an old speculation, and one which, by its very nature, can never be raised above a speculation. This is what is called science! And it is for this that Darwin is lauded to the skies and called blessed among the generations of the devotees of science.

But we would direct attention to another apostle of science—Ernst Hæckel, professor of natural history in the University of Jena. The German naturalist, not satisfied with the assumptions of his English collaborator, advances much further. Taking the theory of evolution as demonstrated, he proceeds to trace out the genealogy of man from his first monad ancestor to his final development into an anthropoid ape, and then into that species of animal that naturalists call *Homo Sapiens*. In his *Natural History of Creation* he boldly and unhesitatingly describes all the links in the chain. Many of these links, of palæozoic antiquity, are represented by animals whose fossil remains, at least, are known to science. Others, however, never have had any existence outside of Hæckel's imagination. But this matters not. Hæckel's theory demands their existence, and that is sufficient reason for their reality. If they have not existed, they ought to have existed. And Hæckel gives all this as veritable science, as the undoubted conclusions of experiment and observation. And more than this: he expects it to be accepted as such—as something that has passed the requirements of demonstration, as something that can no longer be called in question.

But Hæckel does not stop here. He is prepared—men like Hæckel are always prepared for the accomplishment of difficult and impossible tasks—not only to give us a full genealogy of man from the simplest gelatinous monad, but he is also ready to tell how this humble albuminous ancestor of ours was produced from inorganic matter. He does not, of course, believe in a Creator. A belief in God would be anti-scientific, for the reason, Hæckel will tell us, that such a being is unnecessary. According to Hæckel, there exists nothing but matter and force, and these are eternal. Assuming this as unquestionable, he applies his monistic or mechanical theory, and gravely and grandiloquently tells us that all the various forms of organic and inorganic nature are simply the products of natural forces acting on matter. Carbon, hydrogen, oxygen, carbonic acid, and nitrogen, under the multiple action of chemical affinity, electricity, solar heat, and a thousand and one other *unknown* causes, give birth to the simplest forms of animal and vegetable life, and lo! the mystery of creation is explained. As between the exploded theory of spontaneous generation—he calls it *autogenic* archigony—and creation he unhesitatingly accepts the former. Any hypothesis, however wild or absurd it may be, that will enable him to evade admitting the existing of a personal God, Hæckel is prepared to accept and urge on the acceptance of others. He dresses up his theories in an interminable series of neologisms, mostly derived from the Greek, which reminds one of the Macaronic volubility of the doctor of Molière, and, having done this, he fancies, it would seem, that he has marshalled together so many arguments in true syllogistic form.

We challenge any one possessed of the least logical acumen to read Hæckel's *Evolution of Man* or his *History of Creation*, and say that we have been guilty of any exaggeration in the statements we have made regarding his opinions or the artifices to which he has recourse in stating and maintaining them. We do not mean, however, to imply that Hæckel is, as a naturalist, entirely devoid of merit. Far from it. As a patient and acute observer of facts and details, particularly in the domain of the lower forms of invertebrate life, he, like his English co-worker Darwin, is entitled to his meed of praise. But it is when he attempts to generalize from the facts and phenomena observed that Hæckel falls into the most stupid blunders and into the most glaring absurdities.

Hæckel, like Huxley, Tyndall, and Darwin, has written a number of works that have attracted more or less notice. Some of these are monographs of undoubted merit on purely scientific subjects; but those of his productions that have reached the general public are the ones embodying his atheistic views of creation and his flighty imaginings regarding the natural history of animals and man. His observations and discoveries are known only to a few naturalists, whereas the poison of his materialistic teaching has been disseminated, as is usual in such cases, over the whole world.

So much, then, for the four best-known and most popular representatives of modern scientific thought. Huxley and Darwin are not known for their original and extensive researches in biology, but rather for their evolutionary teachings and for their confessed agnosticism. Tyndall is not as much known for his investigations in the domain of physical science as he is for his pronounced materialism. And Hæckel is famous—or infamous, rather—not for his studies of the lower forms of life, but for his theories regarding organic evolution and for his proud and defiant atheism.

And what confirms the truth of what we have been saying, and what at the same time makes matters worse, is the belief in the popular mind—a belief, too, that is more general than most people are disposed to admit—that there is some intimate, if not necessary, connection between the sciences which these men pursue and their avowed irreligious tenets; that their openly-proclaimed agnosticism, materialism, atheism, must, as effect proceeds from cause, follow from their studies of nature and nature's laws. They are looked upon as authoritative teachers, and their utterances on all subjects pertaining to philosophy and religion, no less than those relating to the sciences they profess, are regarded as infallible.

What we have said respecting the four coryphei of modern science just named may with equal truth be iterated of their less eminent but scarcely less notorious disciples. Carl Vogt, and Büchner, and Oscar Schmidt, and Paul Bert take up the teachings of their masters, and carry them, if possible, to even greater extremes. The conclusions they draw are contained, if we will, in the false premises of their teachers; but it is only when the deduction is made that one realizes how terrible and inevitable these conclusions are. They are so wide-reaching that they embrace everything—science, philosophy, morals, religion. Nothing is sacred. And in the teachings of these men we are told that we have embodied the latest deductions of what is popularly known as science—a science that carries with it the subversion of social order, of morality, of religion, and ends with a bold and positive negation of the immortality of the soul and of the existence of a personal God.

According to Büchner, the *natural* origin of man is demonstrated beyond doubt, and has already taken its place among the most memorable discoveries of modern times. From this to the conclusion of Mme. Clémence Royer, one of Darwin's translators, there is but a step. According to this French Darwiness, "Not only motion is transformed into sound, heat, electricity, light, and reciprocally, but all these different forms of one force, which is always identical, are transformed into life, intelligence, will, and voluntary action. . . . Intelligence and thought, like extension, impenetrability, and motion, are simply phenomena of matter." Max Stirner, another member of the same school, sums up his faith more briefly. "There are," he says, "only two realities which I recognize—myself and what I eat." A typical representative indeed of that proud and puffed-up class spoken of by the apostle, that acknowledged " no God but their belly, and whose glory was their shame!"

One would think, to judge from such statements, that the sole object that some of our so-called scientists have in view in the study of nature is the inventing of theories that will exclude God from the universe. But when one peruses the works of such men as Strauss, Vogt, Hæckel, and Büchner one's suspicion becomes a conviction. They declare their real animus, and in terms that cannot be misconstrued, when they avow, as they do, that "To-day, thanks to Darwinism, the torment of the intelligence, meditating on the world and forced to admit finality, is soothed, and aspirations toward a First Cause are calmed. Natural selection has changed all that. It permits one to conceive of an end as unconsciously determined and as infallibly attained, and will replace God for a more happy posterity." Yes, according to Charles Martins, Darwin is "the Messiah of the natural sciences, and Darwinism the gospel of modern times;" or, as Renan would put it, Darwinism is "the grand explanation of the world and of true philosophy."

The danger to be apprehended from these irreligious theories—and it were foolish to close our eyes to it—lies not so much in the errors they embody, but rather in the number of those who, with persistent unanimity, have devoted themselves to the propagation of such theories and the damnable errors with which they are all more or less impregnated. In referring to a similar subject the illustrious Cardinal Newman truly observes that "The world is a collection of individual men, and any one of them may hold and take upon himself to profess un-Christian doctrine, and do his best to propagate it; but few have the power for such a work, or the opportunity. It is by their union into one body, by the intercourse of man with man, and the consequent sympathy thence arising, that error spreads and becomes an authority. Its separate units which make up the body rely upon each other and upon the whole for the truth of their assertions, and thus assumptions and false reasonings are received without question as certain truths on the credit of alternate cheers and appeals and *imprimaturs*."

In what we have said we have given some of the most vaunted conclusions of those who are popularly regarded as the leaders among modern scientists. These conclusions—which, as we shall see, are as unwarranted as they are opposed to the principles of true science—embrace in their final summation the theory of the animal origin of man through organic evolution, and the pernicious atheistic doctrine which recognizes only matter and force.

These conclusions, however, as before stated, are only old errors in a new guise. They are arrayed in a garb demanded by the studies made in the various sciences in these latter days, but the dress used is only a vamped form of an old garment, and the errors which it is designed to adorn, or conceal rather, are only the Protean shapes of the materialism and atheism which were proclaimed by Greek and Roman sophists twenty or thirty centuries ago. Tyndall, Hæckel, Vogt, Büchner, and their school have merely repeated, in modern scientific terminology, the self-same errors that the Doctor of the Gentiles found dominant when he preached in Athens, and which he was called upon to confute when he went to announce the gospel of Christ in the palaces of the Cæsars on the banks of the Tiber.

And yet more. Our modern scientists have not only reiterated the errors that have obtained, in one form or another, for the last three thousand years, but they have also shown themselves just as wanting in unanimity of opinion as did their materialistic and atheistic predecessors of times long past. They agree, it is true, in maintaining what, on final analysis, would prove to be one and the same error—negation of God and free will—but they are not at one as to the way of giving expression to their errors, or as to what should or should not be adduced in support of their impious theories.

Huxley, for instance, like Darwin, is an evolutionist, but he does not at all agree with Darwin in assigning to "natural selection" all that is claimed for it by the plausible author of the *Origin of Species* and of *The Descent of Man*. Hæckel differs from both Huxley and Darwin, and insists on views to which neither of his English co-laborers would subscribe. Indeed, so radical is he, and so gratuitous in his statements, that one will find few among scientists who are not acknowledged disciples of Hæckel, who are prepared to go the same lengths as the professor of Jena. Hæckel coolly draws up the genealogy of man, and pictures for our inspection the different links of the chain from the first monad down to the last ape-man—or, as he puts it, the last pithecanthropoid—and then has the assurance to ask us to give to his fiction the same credence that we should give to the genealogies of the royal families of France or England.

Carl Vogt, one of the high chiefs of evolution, spoke more truthfully than he knew, and certainly with more force than he intended, when he stated that " The discussion respecting the origin of man —a discussion that is characterized by its comparatively slight animation in other civilized countries—has reached its apogee in Germany, and has assumed a character singularly bitter and passionate. There has been a deluge of brochures, verses, and caricatures, even, in which each one overwhelms his adversary with arguments more or less ridiculous, and assails him with opprobious and calumnious epithets. There are two distinct camps: the one under the direction of Mr. Hæckel, who maintains that man is in a direct lineage with the venerable Amphioxus and the Ascidians; whilst M. Semper and his valiant adherents insist on a relationship that is more direct with, and approximates more closely to, the Annelides."

Virchow, the founder of cellular pathology, and Hæckel's teacher, pertinently remarks, in speaking of the theory of evolution, or transformism, as he prefers to call it, that "Rarely does one see a problem as important as transformism treated in a more trifling, I might say more absurd, manner. If to establish a theory it were necessary only to select and combine phenomena after a certain fashion, we might all, whoever we are, quietly sit by our fireside, smoke our cigar, and construct our little theory." In his celebrated address before the German naturalists and physicians at Munich, on "Freedom of Science in the Modern State," he goes further, and declares: "Every positive progress which we have made in the region of prehistoric anthropology has removed us further from the demonstration of this relation." All his more recent utterances, moreover, in reference to the theory of evolution are in accord with this statement. And Du Bois-Reymond, who stands at the head of German physiological science, says, in reference to Hæckel's genesis of man, that his "genealogical trees have, in the eyes of science, about as much value as have the genealogical trees of the heroes of Homer in the eyes of historical criticism."

When, to adduce another instance, it comes to discuss the length of the period of man's existence on earth, the views of our "advanced" scientists and their followers are equally extravagant, and reveal, if anything, a less accordant spirit than that which presides over their speculations concerning man's origin.

The question of man's antiquity has been a favorite one with infidels, materialists, and atheists ever since the time of Voltaire. They seem to imagine that if they can prove the antiquity of man to be greater than that which they have been pleased to find in the Bible, they thereby impugn the truth of the Scriptures, and sap the very foundations of revealed religion. We shall not now indicate wherein lies the falsity of their reasoning, but content ourselves with giving some idea of what persistent and desperate attempts they have made to establish their theories, and how signal, in every case, has been their failure.

The first time the Biblical chronology was seriously called in question was toward the latter part of the last century. The attack was first made in the name of astronomy, and conducted by some of the ablest scientists of the age. Among these were M. Bailly, the distinguished French astronomer, and Prof. Playfair of Edinburgh, one of the most eminent mathematicians of his time. In support of their onslaught they brought forward certain astronomical tables of Hindoo origin, and insisted on it that these tables clearly evinced the fact that observations were made by Hindoo astronomers over four thousand years before the Christian era, and that, consequently, the period of man's existence on earth was much greater than that indicated by the generally received Biblical chronology.

The conclusions, however, of Playfair and Bailly did not stand the test of criticism. The calculations were soon proven to be false, and it was shown that the sacred books of the Hindoos afford no more evidence for the fabled antiquity of man than do the mythical dynasties of China or Babylon.

A few years later, a greater sensation was produced by the discovery of the now famous zodiacs of Esne and Dendarah during the expedition of Napoleon into Egypt. Dupuis, a distinguished French savant, contended that the temples in which these zodiacs were found must be at least fifteen thousand years old. Other investigators were content with an antiquity of twelve thousand years. Many scientists were now sure that they had evidence that could not be questioned, and infidels boastfully proclaimed that the Christian chronology might be set aside as a myth. But just at the most heated period of the discussion— a discussion in which the whole civilized world was interested—the illustrious Champollion, the discoverer of the hieroglyphical alphabet of ancient Egypt, came forward and proved to a certainty that the much-vaunted zodiacs referred to schemes of nativity in connection with judicial astrology, and belonged to a period not antecedent to the first and second centuries of the Christian era.

Disconcerted and worsted in their astronomical campaign, the forces of error and their scientific allies, although loth to acknowledge defeat, prepared at once to reconnoitre for a coigne of vantage in a more propitious and less accessible field. They soon found the object of their quest in the new and then unexplored domains of geology and prehistoric archæology. Unable to cope with the soldiers of truth on the broad, open plain and in the clear light of the suns and constellations of heaven, the enemies of revelation and of true science betook themselves to the dark and tangled forests of the mountain fastnesses. Here they at once began a guerilla warfare with weapons of an entirely different character from those which they had previously used, and with these they flattered themselves that they would soon march to certain victory.

One squad would get behind a shell-mound and assail its enemies with the calcareous remains of cockles and periwinkles; another would entrench itself in some gravel-pit, and thence hurl a shower of flint arrows and palæolithic javelins; and still another would seek concealment in some weird, damp, gloomy cave, and from the darkness thereof project the fragmentary bones of extinct bears, hyenas, and pachyderms, and occasionally, too, in the way of a *coup de grace*, the ghastly cranium of some hapless mortal who, in an age long past, had died and found his final resting-place in this self-same cavern.

To pass from the language of figure to the language of fact, the argument, briefly stated, was this: Researches in the dim and prehistoric past, and notably in the fertile fields of anthropology, have brought to light a number of facts that, as contended by a certain school of scientists and a still more numerous school of infidel sciolists, prove unquestionably that man's antiquity must be much greater than any rational interpretation of Scripture would permit one to assign.

The evidence in support of the argument comes in the form of ancient human remains and human implements and monuments which recently have been discovered, and about which much has been said and written. We are referred to fossil remains of man found buried deep in the solid rock, the formation of which above and around the remains found must, we are informed, have required untold ages—periods of time that can be reckoned only by tens of thousands of years. We are told of the fossil man of Guadalupe, found embedded in the shell and coral limestone of Guadalupe in the West Indies; of the fossil man of Denise, discovered under a lava deposit from an extinct volcano in Auvergne, France; of the fossil man of Mentone, in Italy; of the skulls of Cro-Magnon and Neanderthal, and of fossil remains of like character found in various parts of the Old and of the New World. We are forced to listen to learned disquisitions on the round towers of Ireland; on the weems and burghs and pillar-stones of Scotland; on the rock-cut temples of India and Arabia Petra; and the no less famous structures and monuments of Central America and Yucatan. We are overwhelmed with the relics of ancient Swiss lake-dwellings and Danish kitchen-middings, and are compelled to inspect specimens, whose number is legion, from all the bone-caves and peat and gravel deposits of Europe; and all this because some theorist, forsooth—some scientific monomaniac, we should say—will have it that he has found in some peculiarly shaped flints, that might have been fashioned by the action of the elements themselves, as well as by human hands, or in some piece of pottery, an irrefragable argument in support of his notion of the fabled antiquity of his ancestors, who, by the way, he will just as strongly insist, are in a direct line of descent from some extinct family of anthropomorphous apes. It is indeed a pity that we cannot consistently tell such an one that we believe him, and that, in *his* case at least, we are disposed to accept his conclusions as the expression of the truth.

But let us give the results, expressed in numbers, of some of the conclusions of a few of our popular geologists and anthropologists respecting the antiquity of man.

The illustrious naturalist Count Pourtales finds fossil human remains in a fresh-water sandstone in Florida, and Prof. Louis Agassiz forthwith estimates them to be "by a moderate computation" 10,000 years old. A certain Mr. Horner comes across some piece of pottery and burnt bricks at various depths in the mud deposits of the Nile, and makes calculations—in which Sir John Lubbock and Sir Charles Lyell substantially agree—which require for man an antiquity of at least 13,000 years. Other geologists, by computations based on these same pieces of pottery and burnt bricks, will extend the 13,000 to 60,000 years. Jukes, an English geologist, puts the antiquity of the human period at 100,000 years. According to Lyell and Lubbock, palæolithic man must date back some 200,000 years. Prof. Fuhlrott makes an exhaustive study of the Neanderthal skull—a human cranium that attracted an immense deal of attention at the time of its discovery—and claims for it an antiquity of from 200,000 to 300,000 years. Mr. Vivian, another geologist, from certain fossils discovered in a cave in Devonshire, estimates the duration of the human period in England at 264,000 years. Subsequently these figures were extended to 1,000,000. Dr. Hunt, at one time president of the British Anthropological Society, thinks that Mr. Vivian's estimate, high as it is, is insufficient. He goes to work and figures the antiquity of our race to be full 9,000,000 years.

Again, many geologists, among them Mr. James Geik, contend that man existed before the Glacial Period, the beginning of which, according to Mr. James Croll, the astronomer, dates back 240,000 years. Scientists, however, are not at one in their estimates of either the date or the duration of the Glacial Period. Mr. Evan Hopkins, F.G.S., says that there are geologists who place back the beginning of the Glacial Age at 1,280,000,000 years. If, then, man is pre-glacial, according to these geologists, he has an antiquity before which the age claimed for him by Manetho, Berosus, and Sanchoniathon in their dynasties of Egypt, Babylon, and Phœnicia, fall into insignificance. Even the countless and everlasting dynasties of the Chinese can produce nothing that will give man a more truly venerable antiquity than the estimates given by the geologists just mentioned.

But enough of such figures and surmises. We wish to know what foundation in fact there is for such conjectures respecting the antiquity of our race, why there is such a wide divergence in the results obtained, and what conclusions have been reached by more conservative although equally eminent investigators, and what, in a word, are the views of Christian and Catholic savants regarding this most interesting question.

All, or nearly all, conclusions like those indicated are based, as we already have stated, on calculations concerning the age of human remains and human implements, etc., to some of which we have just alluded. The marked divergence in the results obtained is owing to the lack, in most cases, of any reliable means of determining, even approximately, the age of the objects found. The age of a human bone, or of any kind of implement of human fabrication, is ordinarily arrived at by computing the amount of time necessary to form the deposits, be they of rock, mud, or peat, in which such human remains are found.

Let us illustrate by a case in point. Some forty years ago, M. Boucher de Perthes, a French savant, discovered a large number of articles of human fabrication in the peat deposits of the valley of the Somme, in France. His discoveries were so startling, and gave, according to his interpretation of them, such a great antiquity to the human race, that at first they were received with distrust on all sides. They did not, however, attract any special attention from scientists generally until about the year 1860.

According to M. Boucher de Perthes' measurements, the peat in which the articles referred to were found was formed at the rate of about an inch and a half or two inches a century. Sir Charles Lyell, Sir John Lubbock, and other well-known scientists, after making an extended examination of these same peat-beds and the objects found therein, were disposed to accept M. Boucher de Perthes' estimate concerning the rate of formation of the peat, and to regard the various objects found in it as having a very great antiquity indeed. In some places the peat mentioned had a depth of twenty-six feet, and must therefore, according to M. Boucher de Perthes and Lyell and Lubbock, have required for its formation a period embracing from fifteen to twenty thousand years.

But we can appreciate better the trustworthiness of such observations and computations by comparisons with discoveries made in similar formations elsewhere.

In the catalogue of the antiquities in the museum of the Royal Irish Academy we are told of a leather shoe found twenty feet below the surface in a peat-bog in Tipperary. In the same catalogue mention is made of a large vessel of butter discovered in the turf at the depth of eighteen feet, in the county of Kilkenny. If, then, we are to believe M. Boucher de Perthes and Sir Charles Lyell and Sir John Lubbock, and scientists of their stamp, the Irish were wearing leather shoes and making butter upward of ten or twelve thousand years ago. *Risum teneatis amici.*

We may add, in this connection, that sober and more extended observation has shown that peat can be and has been formed at a much more rapid rate than that assigned by the geologists just named. There are well-authenticated instances of peat being formed at the rate of a foot or two, or even more, per century. Dr. Andrews and others who have taken up the subject of the peat deposits of the Somme valley maintain that a careful investigation will prove that the time demanded for their formation has been greatly exaggerated. Four or five thousand years is the maximum of time they are disposed to allow, and they think that half that time is amply sufficient.

In the same way eminent geologists and archæologists, whose authority and erudition cannot be questioned, cut down the exaggerated estimates that have been given to the Glacial Period and to the age of the various human remains that have been found, and to that of the divers works of art and industry that have been attributed to prehistoric man. Instead of the hundreds of thousands or millions of years that have been assigned to the human period, it has been demonstrably shown that there is no valid reason for claiming for it an antiquity greater than eight or ten thousand years at most. In other words, so far as any positive knowledge in geology and prehistoric archæology goes, these sciences can make no claims that are in conflict with the general statements of Scripture regarding the age of our race.

The trouble in geology is that we have no chronometers, no means of reckoning time in years, no positive *data* that can serve as units of measure. All geological calculations expressed in years are simply guesses—conjectures, more or less probable, more or less fanciful and extravagant. But it is only among Christian geologists that we observe a disposition to acknowledge the full force of the difficulty. Geologists of infidel and materialistic tendencies are loath to admit that the lack of some unit of measure is sufficient to vitiate all their calculations. They still insist that their computations, however diverse, and notwithstanding the long periods of time required, must be right, because, as they will have it, the Bible, with its cosmogony, genealogies, and all, is wrong. Truly, it requires faith more than sufficient to move mountains to be an infidel or modern scientist in good standing.

The great American, and, we may add, Christian geologist, J. D. Dana, who occupies an undisputed place in the front rank of the great geologists of the age, makes no attempt to determine the number of years that go to make up any of the epochs or periods that geology speaks of, but simply limits himself to the statement of the general proposition, "Time is long."

M. A. de Lapparent, the eminent Catholic geologist, in his recent admirable *Traité de Géologie*, said to be the most complete and reliable work on geology extant, declares that the data on which the geologist is obliged to rely "are so vague that, according to the point of view which one adopts, the figures may vary from one to twenty; sometimes from one to a hundred; and yet even these extreme results deserve scarcely more credence than the others. Wherefore we must accept with the greatest reserve the numerical results which divers authors pretend to have attained."

But physics and astronomy furnish us with still stronger reasons for withholding assent to the gratuitous assumptions and exorbitant demands made by a certain class of geologists and biologists for the unlimited secular periods which their speculations require. Instead of the hundreds of millions of years demanded by the advocates of evolution, Sir William Thompson—now Lord Kelvin—and P. G. Tait, who are conceded to be without superiors in their special lines of research, tell us that calculations based on the laws of thermodynamics—something much more trustworthy than the data geologists have to compute from—prove that it would have been simply impossible for any form of animal or vegetable life to have existed on the earth for a greater period of time than ten, or, at most, fifteen, million years.

Unlike the results reached by geologists, we here have conclusions that are based on measurable units and calculable quantities. We have a mathematical problem resting on experimental data of physics, and the answer to this problem affords us an argument against the unwarranted deductions of geologists that is simply irrefutable.

In a lecture delivered a few years ago before the Royal Institution in London, Sir William Thompson emphasized the conclusions he had previously arrived at, and, applying to the discussion of the sun's heat the same methods he had employed in the problem respecting the thermal condition and age of the earth, he declared that it is impossible "to suppose that the sun has existed for more than twenty million years, no matter what may have been its origin—whether it came into existence from the clash of worlds pre-existing or from diffused nebulous matter." "There is," he says, "a great clinging by geologists and biologists to vastly longer periods, but the physicist, treating it"—viz. the duration of solar and terrestrial heat—"as a dynamic question, with calculable elements, cannot come to any other conclusion than the one stated."

Mr. H. Faye, one of the ablest astronomers of the age, and a Catholic, goes even farther, and draws up an argument that is, if anything, more trenchant than that of either Thompson or Tait. In his masterly work *Sur l'Origine du Monde*, he states it as his belief, founded on well-known physical and astronomical laws, that the sun—assuming the amount of heat annually radiated by it to have been the same since its formation as it is now—cannot possibly have a greater age than 14,500,000 years. To this he adds, what must strike every one as unquestionable, that, for those who admit the nebular hypothesis of Laplace—and most geologists and biologists pin their faith to this hypothesis—the difficulties presented by the results of his calculations to the acceptance of the long life-periods which geologists claim are simply insoluble.

The errors and the changing and contradictory opinions we have referred to regarding the antiquity of man, and, incidentally, the life-period of the earth, are not, however, restricted to this special subject of investigation. On the contrary, they obtain, even in a more marked degree, if that be possible, in every other department of what is currently denominated " modern science." We have the same cloud of error and conflicting opinion enveloping subjects that are most intimately associated with the gravest questions of philosophy and theology. This is particularly true of such problems as those concerning the origin and nature of man, the unity of species, and other problems of an equally vital nature embraced in the general theory of evolution. But we have not space to discuss these questions now, for they would each require far more than could be allotted them. Indeed, each would afford abundant material for a separate article. But, if examined, they would only tend to confirm what has already been demonstrated. Let it suffice for the present to have alluded to them. From what has been said so far in the course of this chapter, we can see what we are called upon to accept as science. We have learned also, *en passant*, something of those who would present themselves as our teachers and as the exponents of the "new philosophy."

"Modern science, then,"—we refer to the sham science we have been considering—is nothing more than the vain and idle imaginings of those who, in the language of Tertullian, "fail to see that which is, and imagine that which is not." It is a science "garrulous, declaiming, canting, wrangling;" a science barren of useful things, and "meanly proud of its own unprofitableness." It is a fuming, frothing, vaporing gushing of words, and an incoherent syllabling and mouthing of names, as dauntless in its effrontery as it is persistent in its attempts to hoist and foist itself into the elevated and sacred shrines of true science and true philosophy. It ends, as has been said of the sophistry of the Greeks, in nothing but disputation and incertitude. "It is neither a vineyard nor an olive-ground, but an intricate wood of briers and thistles, from which those who lose themselves in it bring back many scratches and no food." It is, in a word, simply a continuation in a new form, and with variations, of the futile and trifling "disputes of the orthodox Lilliputians and the heretical Blefuscudians about the big ends and the little ends of eggs."

As to the high priests and expositors of this so-called science, we can say of them, in the language of Macaulay, that "we have been for some time past inclined to suspect that these people, whom some regard as the lights of the world and others as incarnate demons, are in general ordinary men, with narrow understandings and little information." We can apply to them, each according to his measure, what Ruskin says in his own telling language of that much-overrated naturalist Charles Darwin: "He attracts the attention only of vainly curious and idly skeptical persons, and has collected in the train of him every impudent imbecility in Europe, like a dim comet wagging its useless tail of phosphorescent nothing across the steadfast stars."

Yes, these exponents of modern science—more particularly its German and French representatives —will flippantly talk of our gaseous and albuminoid ancestors, and express surprise if one should venture to dissent from any of their views, however extravagant. They will deny the glorious origin of the human family as declared in the Book of books, and then work with the incessancy and malignity and desperation of a Mephistopheles to show that man, the lord of creation, descends in a direct line from some favored worm or sea-squirt, from some privileged mud-fish or catarrhine ape. They will prate glibly about the souls of animals and plants, and insist on our denying the immortality of our own. They will ask us to give up our faith and plunge with them into the maelstrom of materialism or an all-absorbing pantheism; and in lieu of those sacred truths on which have ever been based the hope, the joy, the consolation of our race, they will offer us in return a dark, cold, forbidding atheism. In the words of the poet,

> "They cast on all things surest, sweetest, best,
> Doubt, insecurity, astonishment."

CHAPTER IV.

THE FRIENDS AND THE FOES OF SCIENCE.

REVIEWING the history of the past as written during the last few decades, we shall find that many important chapters have been entirely revised, and that numerous statements which a German writer has well characterized as "historical lies" have been rejected as never having had any foundation in fact. The chapter concerning the inductive sciences, and especially the relation of these sciences to the Church and to those who have been in communion with the Church, is yet to be written. We want a historian who can distinguish true from false science; who can discriminate between theory and doctrine; who, in a word, can point out to us who are the real friends and who are the real foes of science.

If we look over the field of science to-day, we shall find that the so-called leaders of modern thought would have us accept the flimsiest hypotheses and wildest speculations as the unquestionable ultimate results of scientific investigation. We shall discover also that these alleged "advanced thinkers" are men without faith, and generally men who deny the existence of God. We shall see, too, that they are popular, and that their theories are popular, because they are sensational and because they run counter to the traditional teachings of our race, and more particularly because they are opposed to the truths of revelation and the positive doctrines of the Catholic Church. A glance will tell us of the lack of unanimity in the conclusions reached by these popular and applauded representatives of science; that they differ as much from one another as to what is scientific truth as do the same class of exponents of science of one age differ from those of the age succeeding.

If we extend our view back beyond the "living present," and consult the records of the past, we shall learn that the most energetic and successful workers in every department of science, and the greatest champions of progress, were those who were the most devoted sons of Holy Church and the most consistent believers in her teachings. The friends of the Church, of revelation, of sound doctrine, have ever been the friends of true science. On the other hand, science has known no greater foes than those who have actively opposed the Church, denied her dogmas, or called in question her divine origin.

In view of these undeniable historic facts, we shall in this chapter, discuss the principles that give rise to such conflicting opinions, such false and sensational conclusions. We shall inquire why it is that men of ability, as many of our scientific professors unquestionably are, fall into such egregious errors and ridiculous absurdities. And, finally, we shall show, in the light of history, what a spirit of intolerance has ever reigned outside of the Catholic Church—a spirit as intolerant of true science as of Catholic dogma; a spirit that has been as antagonistic to scientific progress as it has been to the propagation of the gospel; a spirit, too, which has headed a persecution as bitter and as protracted in matters of science as any recorded in the annals of religious intolerance.

One need not, indeed, be surprised at finding those who are outside of the Church falling into error regarding the various subjects with which the scientist is supposed to deal. Conflicting errors and changing opinions are the inevitable results consequent on rejecting the Church's authority. The theories and the guesses, the materialism and the atheism, which go so far toward making up what is known as "modern science" are simply the natural outgrowth of the great apostacy of the sixteenth century.

The German "Reformers," with Luther at their head, rejected the Church and retained the Bible; the Deists of England cast away the Bible and held on to God; the Encyclopædiasts of France repudiated God and contracted their faith to a simple recognition of the existence of matter.

Luther opposed Catholicity; Voltaire battled against Christianity; modern materialism has entered the lists against religion of every form. The pantheists of the last century insisted on it that all men are gods. The materialists of our own age are equally positive that we are all beasts. At one time scientists, with Lalande, will refuse to believe in the existence of God because they have never seen Him with their telescopes; at any other time they will join in a chorus of praise about "Father Mud, the Almighty Plastic." With Broussais, they deny that there is a soul because, forsooth, they have never found it at the end of their scalpels; and, with La Mettrie, they teach that man is merely a plant or a machine. In one generation "everything," in the words of Bossuet, "is God except God Himself; and in another, men who call themselves scientists will write long treatises on nature without even a mention of the name of Deity, and without the slightest allusion to His power and wisdom as displayed in His works. With Hæckel, they will believe in spontaneous generation, although it has been proven to be absurd, rather than acknowledge the miracle of creation. In a word, "Every one of them," to quote the language of Voltaire, "destroys and renovates the earth after his own fashion, as Descartes framed it; for philosophers put themselves without ceremony in the place of God, and think they can create a universe with a word."

But our modern "advanced thinkers" have gone even further. Not content with eliminating from their creed everything pertaining to theology, they have gone so far as to discard logic and philosophy. They sneer at the productions of the great masters of thought of ancient and mediæval times, and speak of their philosophic labors in terms of undisguised contempt.

Büchner, for instance, flippantly declares that the metaphysics of the Platos, the Descarteses, the Malebranches, the Bossuets, the Fenelons, the Leibnitzes, and the Clarkes may beguile simple minds, but no one, like himself presumably, could seriously regard it as a science.

With Büchner, as with modern scientists generally outside of the pale of the Church, everything is reduced to induction, and it is applied indiscriminately to the discussion of every question, whether of the natural or of the supernatural order. According to them, a man cannot consistently profess a belief in the truths of philosophy as a science of principles and at the same time be a scientist.

In his work on *Man in the Past, Present, and Future* Büchner quotes, as expressing his own sentiments and those of his school, the violent denunciations of the atheistic Dr. Page against all who have the hardihood to accept anything which, like the truths of philosophy or religion, presupposes fixedness and unchangeableness of belief.

"No man," says Dr. Page, "who has subscribed to creeds and formulæ, whether in theology or philosophy, can be an unbiased investigator of the truth or an unprejudiced judge of the opinions of others. His sworn preconceptions warp his discernment; adherence to his sect or party engenders intolerance to the honest convictions of other inquirers. Beliefs we may and must have, but a belief to be changed with new and advancing knowledge impedes no progress, while a creed subscribed to as ultimate truth, and sworn to be defended, not only puts a bar to further research, but as a consequence throws the odium of distrust on all that may seem to oppose it. Even when such odium cannot deter, it annoys and irritates; hence the frequent unwillingness of men of science to come prominently forward with the avowal of their beliefs. It is time this delicacy were thrown aside, and such theologians plainly told that the skepticism and infidelity, if skepticism and infidelity there be, lies all on their own side. There is no skepticism so offensive as that which doubts the facts of honest and careful observations; no infidelity so gross as that which disbelieves the deductions of competent and unbiased judgments."

And "these words of gold," to which Büchner and his associates say amen, " deserve to be graven on brass and affixed to the doors of all churches, schools, and editorial rooms."

It would be indeed difficult to put in words

more damning evidence in support of the arraignment we have drawn up against modern scientists than the passages we have just quoted. Nothing could reveal more clearly their methods or declare more explicitly their desires and purposes. Passion and zeal in furtherance of an ungodly cause have led them to make known the animus that governs them in their researches, and to betray the secret of the subterfuges and tergiversations that characterize them, and of the pronounced hostility they display whenever there is question of the relation of science to the Church.

As to a Catholic scientist, it would be simply impossible for him to fall into the errors, contradictions, and absurdities of those who have rejected the assistance and guidance of reason and faith, of philosophy and revelation. He would not idle away his time in futile speculations which his faith, if not his reason, would tell him have no foundation in fact. On the contrary, he would eschew all such sources of error, and be spared the mortification of the constant changes and retractions our modern materialistic scientists are ever obliged to make.

In his admirable *Sept Leçons de Physique Générale*, the immortal Cauchy, conceded to be the ablest mathematician of his age, makes a pointed reference to this subject. Speaking of the precautions that students of science should take to avoid falling into error, he says: "One ought to reject without hesitation every hypothesis which is in contradiction to revealed truth. I do not say this in the interests of religion, but in the interests of science, because truth can never contradict itself. It is for having neglected this rule that there have been scientists who have squandered in futile attempts much precious time that might have been happily employed in making useful discoveries. What important contributions might not have been made to our collection of scientific memoirs if religion had always guided the pen of those authors who, for a while, imagined that they had discovered that the zodiacs of Denderah and Esne have an antiquity of twelve thousand years; that man is descended from a polyp; that he has existed on earth from all eternity; that the Deluge is a fable; that the creation of man and animals was the effect of chance; that even in our own days they can be seen springing from the earth in the isles of the great ocean; and that the natives of America form a different species from that to which we belong, etc.! Yes, gentlemen," the learned author continues, "we are forced to recognize the fact that, as in regulating the heart of man and interdicting to him false pleasures, religion simply opens up to him a new source of ineffable joys and seeks his own happiness, so also, in imposing on the mind of the savant certain rules, she simply confines his imagination within just limits, and spares him the regret of having been misled by false systems and pernicious illusions."

The lesson here inculcated is the one put in practice by every Catholic student of science. It is, indeed, one of the most striking characteristics of the many eminent men who have reflected honor on science and the Church that they have always known what are the true limits of science as distinguished from those of philosophy and theology, and that they have understood how to steer clear of the Scylla and Charybdis that have been the destruction of so many proud and venturesome spirits outside of the Church.

The distinguished French chemist M. Berthelot, in writing to M. Renan *apropos* of this subject, says: " Positive science pursues neither first causes nor the end of things, but it proceeds by establishing facts and connecting them with each other by intimate relations. . . . The human mind ascertains the facts by observation and experience; it compares them, and thence infers relations; that is to say, facts which are more general. These in turn—and this is the sole guarantee of their reality —are verified by observation and experience. It is the chain of these relations, extended further each day by the efforts of human intelligence, that constitutes positive science."

In referring to the same subject the eminent physiologist Claude Bernard declares that "First causes are not within the domain of science; they always escape us, as well in the science of living bodies as in the science of brute matter."

The celebrated Pasteur says, in the same strain, that "Experimental science is essentially positivist in this sense, that in its conceptions it never introduces the consideration of the essence of things, of the origin of the world and of its destinies."

Were we to question the other great representatives of science, of present or past time, concerning the domain of the sciences in which they achieved such success, they would give us the same answer.* With Cauchy, Berthelot, Claude Bernard, Pasteur, they would tell us that science deals simply with facts and phenomena; that the

* It gives us pleasure to quote here from two of the most renowned, although two much neglected, scientists of the Middle Ages—viz. Roger Bacon and Albertus Magnus, the former a Franciscan monk, the latter a Dominican friar. To these eminent scholars and to Galileo, of a later age, and not to Lord Bacon, is due the introduction of the inductive or experimental method in the natural and physical sciences. Roger Bacon, in his *Opus Majus*, p. vi. 1, says: "Duo sunt modi cognoscendi, scilicet per argumentum et experientiam. Sine experientia nihil sufficienter sciri potest. Argumentum concludit sed non certificat, neque removet dubitationem ut quiescat animus in intuitu veritatis, nisi eam inveniat via experientiæ." Albertus Magnus, *Opp.*, tom. v. p. 340, writes: "Harum autem, quas ponemus, quasdam quidem ipsi nos experimento probavimus, quasdam autem referimus ex dictis eorum, quos comperimus non de facile aliqua dicere nisi probata per experimentum. Experimentum enim solum certificat de talibus, eo quod de tam particularibus syllogismus haberi non potest."

methods and instruments of the scientist cannot be applied to questions that belong to an order that is supersensible or supernatural. Ever ready to acknowledge the assistance afforded by philosophy and revealed truth, and to recognize the light they throw on the many complicated questions which arise in the study of nature, they yet always have before them the lines of demarcation separating the sciences based on induction from those that repose on the firmer and more certain bases of reason and faith.

It has been such men, working in accordance with the principles indicated, who have given to the world the precious deposit of science it now possesses; and it is one of the glories of the Church that she can point to all the great masters of true science as those who, if not in every instance within her pale, were trained in accordance with her teachings, and were ever, directly or indirectly, under her influence. She has always counted, and still counts, among her children the most eminent representatives of every department of science. Wherever there is question of original, practical work as distinguished from distracting, fickle theorizing, her children are the first to respond to the call.

But, as a rule, this is a kind of work of which the world hears little or nothing. There is nothing sensational about it—nothing that, as a rule, will secure fame, much less notoriety, for those who engage in it. It has not about it that glamour of novelty, that fascination of presentation, which so captivates the superficial multitude in the speculations of Darwin, Huxley, Tyndall, Hæckel, and others of their school. It is, however, just such work as is accomplished by these quiet, unassuming laborers in the fields of science that is appropriated for the construction of the various new-fangled hypotheses of which we hear so much.

And here, indeed, lies the great distinction between the two classes of scientists of whom we have been speaking. Those who are directly or indirectly under the influence of the Church are eminently practical men—men of fact, of patient research, of rigid demonstration; men who will accept nothing as science that is not proven, and will entertain nothing as scientifically possible that contravenes any of the acknowledged truths of philosophy or revelation. Those, however, who boast of being free-thinkers—who are intellectually the lineal descendants of the proud, independent, self-sufficient spirits of the apostacy of the sixteenth century—the agnostics, materialists, and atheists to whom we have referred during the course of this chapter—are men who instinctively prefer, whatever they may aver to the contrary, fancy to fact, hypothesis to demonstration, theory to positive science. They are, in a word, men who wish to have a world without a God, and they bend all their energies to devise plausible arguments to deceive themselves and those who, like themselves, are seeking for some pretext for being deceived. Only on this assumption can we account for the amazing popularity of the anti-religious theories of certain modern scientists who, in reality, have nothing to offer except simple negation of all that is grand and noble in religion and philosophy.

"By their fruits ye shall know them." We may compare the representatives of the two schools—the Catholic and the non-Catholic, the Christian and the anti-Christian—and we shall find that even in those departments of science in which the latter boast of having accomplished so much it is to the former that justice must decree the award for meritorious work. Instances that prove the truth of this assertion abound in every period of the history of science.

Among some of the many who are now distinguished, or who in recent years have been distinguished, for their eminence in science and for their loyalty to Holy Church may be mentioned Leverrier, Faye, and Fathers Secchi, Denza, Ferrari, Perry, Searle, and Hagen among astronomers; the brothers Tulasne and Edward L. Greene among botanists; Barrande, Gaudry, Dumont, d'Homalius d'Halloy, Collet, de Lapparent, de la Vallée Poussin, and Charles Sainte-Claire Deville among geologists; Barf, Renard, Dumas, Berthelot, Chevreul, and Henri Sainte-

Claire Deville among chemists; Chasles, Pussieux, Cauchy, Gilbert, and Hermite among mathematicians; General Newton, Count de Lesseps, and Eiffel, of Eiffel-tower fame, among engineers; Schwann, Johannes Müller, St. George Mivart, Claude Bernard, Canon Carnoy, Van Beneden, and Pasteur among zoölogists and comparative anatomists; the abbés Hamard, Delaunay, Bourgeois, Ducrost, Arcelin, Cau Durban, Béroud, and the Marquis de Nadaillac among prehistoric archæologists. These illustrious men, faithful sons of the Church and deserving well of science, have simply kept the traditions of their eminent predecessors in similar departments of science.

And what has been said of those just enumerated can also be affirmed of many distinguished Christian scientists who, nominally without the fold of the Church, have never strayed far away from her benign influence. Among the numbers who, during the last generation, have added lustre to science and borne witness to the truth of Christian teaching we may count the names of James Clerk Maxwell, Gabriel Stokes, P. G. Tait, Sir William Thompson, Asa Gray, J. D. Dana, Quaterfages, Dawson, Joseph Henry, Fresnel, Liebig, Mayer, Sir David Brewster, Dr. Whewell, Adam Sedgwick, Sir Roderick Murchison, E. Hitchcock, Sir John Herschell, and Michael Faraday. And should we wish to go back further, we should find such men as Copernicus, Galileo,

Sir Isaac Newton, Cuvier, Euler, Leibnitz, Linnæus, Kepler, Hugh Miller, Davy, Volta, Galvani, Ampère, Oerstedt, Pascal, Descartes, and a host of others scarcely inferior to them in genius and the extent of their attainments who were as staunch defenders of revealed truth as they were valiant champions of science.

The Church, then, does not impede the progress of science. Her influence has not been of that blighting sort that her enemies are so fond of ascribing to her. On the contrary, the names mentioned—and it were easy to increase the list—are sufficient evidence of the falsity of the charge. Her standing in the scientific world to-day, represented as she is by the most brilliant minds in every department of human thought; her past history in reference to the development of science and the fostering care which she has always bestowed upon those who devoted themselves to the study of nature, are an irrefragable argument for the validity of the position she has ever assumed, and still maintains, respecting the relations of the science of nature to reason and revelation.

We have already seen what has been the outcome, in their bearing on science, of the principles adopted and promulgated by the so-called reformers of the sixteenth century. The principles of Luther and Calvin and Zuinglius and Bucer have been carried out to their logical consequences by their followers, and we have to-day, as their representatives and lineal descendants in Germany, the Hæckels, the Vogts, the Büchners, the Strauses, the Schmidts, the Schopenhauers, and their legions of co-laborers and sympathizers. In France the teachings of the Reformation are to be seen in the works of such authors as Renan, Madame Royer, and Paul Bert; and in England in the productions of Spencer, Darwin, Huxley, and Tyndall.

Yet, notwithstanding all the evidence to the contrary, a certain class of writers still indulge in the fancy of referring to the Reformation as the one great event in the world's history that liberated mankind from the intellectual thralldom with which it had so long been oppressed by the Church of Rome. Science, they tell us, was then given free scope, something it never had in the past, and men of science rejoiced in a liberty that they had long sighed for, but had never known before. We have seen what are now the fruits of this liberty—a liberty that means materialism of the rankest kind and atheism of the most pronounced character.

But was science given the free scope about which there has been so much boasting? Were men of science encouraged, and did the Reformation contribute to the advancement of science? This is a question of history, and to history we appeal for an answer.

We may quote, as authority, one who has always shown himself specially inimical to the Church, and whose testimony, therefore, cannot be called in question by his fellow anti-Catholics. We refer to J. W. Draper. In his *History of the Conflict between Science and Religion*—a conflict, by the way, that has never existed so far as the Church is concerned—the author, in speaking of the effect of the Reformation on scientific development, says: "Luther declared that the study of Aristotle is wholly useless; his vilification of the Greek philosopher knew no bounds. 'He is,' says Luther, 'truly a devil, a horrid calumniator, a wicked sycophant, a prince of darkness, a real Apollyon, a beast, a most horrid impostor on mankind, one in whom there is scarcely any philosophy, a public and professed liar, a goat, a complete epicure, this twice execrable Aristotle.' The schoolmen were, as Luther said, 'locusts, caterpillars, frogs, lice.' He entertained an abhorrence of them. These opinions, though not so emphatically expressed, were entertained by Calvin. *So far as science is concerned, nothing is owed to the Reformation.*"

When Luther comes to speak of universities and schools, his language is nothing short of the ravings of demoniac frenzy. Any one who will take the trouble to consult any of the earlier editions of his complete works—the later editions are more or less expurgated—can verify for himself the accuracy of this statement. "Universities," according to Luther, "are dens of robbers, temples of Moloch, synagogues of perdition. All high schools,". said he, "should be razed to the ground. Nothing more infernal or more diabolical has ever come or ever will come upon the earth." He regarded them as the works of the devil, and said that "during the reign of the popes the devil spread his nets to catch the souls of men by the erection of schools and convents."

But let us come to facts and figures bearing on the influence of the preachments of Luther and his coadjutors on the study and progress of science.

The dean of the philosophical faculty of the University of Erfurt, in an official report for the year 1523, says: "No one living before our day would have believed it, if it had been foretold him, that in a short time our universities would have fallen so low—as they have fallen—that there would scarcely remain a shadow of their former glory. The subject of the university is so treated in the pulpits of the Reformers that there is scarcely anything connected with it which erstwhile was held in estimation that is not now condemned." *

From year to year, after the introduction of the Reformation, the number of teachers and students

---

* For the quotations here made, see the admirable *Geschicte des Deutschen Volkes zeit dem Ausgang des Mittelalters*, von Johannes Janssen, Band 2, p. 294 *et seq.*

at Erfurt rapidly decreased. More than this: it soon became difficult to find proper persons who cared to accept a position in any capacity either in this or other universities or schools.

The number of students matriculated at Erfurt from 1520 to 1521 was 311. In the following year the number sank to 120; in 1522 it fell to 72; and in the year 1523-4 there remained only 34.

The fate of Wittenberg was the same as that of Erfurt. Melanchthon, the least vandalic of the Reformers, and the one who displayed the greatest love of learning, does not hesitate, in his confidential correspondence, to attribute the decline of science and the contempt in which studies of all kinds were held to the Reformed theologians. He declares that "the age has become an age of iron, that the sciences are neglected and despised," and that he despairs of any revival in their behalf.

The universities of Northern Germany, as Leipsic and Rostock, fared no better. In Rostock, which before the Reformation counted full 300 students, the number in 1524 had dwindled down to 38, and in the year following the roll-call was responded to by only 15.

The same sad picture was presented in South Germany and Switzerland, and notably at Heidelberg, Freiburg, and Basle. "The University seems dead and buried," was the wail that went out from Basle in 1524. "The rostrums of professors and the benches of students are empty."

In the year 1522 it could count only 29 students, and in the year 1526 the number enrolled was 5.

Heidelberg in 1525 numbered more professors than students. "I have now only six students, and these are French." Thus wrote from Freiburg, in 1523, the most celebrated professor of jurisprudence of his age, Ulrich Zasius.

Under the Emperor Maximilian I. the University of Vienna had attained to the rank of one of the most celebrated institutions of learning in Europe. It then counted its professors by the hundred, and frequently had a yearly attendance of 7000 students. But this happy condition of things was soon to undergo a melancholy change. In consequence of the religious disturbances and social disorder induced by the Reformation, matters shortly came to such a pass that the attendance was reduced to scarcely a dozen, and the lecture-halls of the law faculty had to be closed for want of students.

What has been said of the universities mentioned may, to a greater or less extent, be said of all the educational institutions where the Reformation was able to gain a foothold. It had the same blighting effect in Holland as it had in Germany and Switzerland. The decline of science and letters followed its entrance into Scandinavia, and a protracted period of scientific drought was consequent on its introduction into England and Scotland.

Speaking of Catholicity in England before the period of the Reformation, Cobbett declares: "There were in those times nearly three hundred halls and private schools at Oxford, besides the colleges, and there were not above eight remaining toward the middle of the seventeenth century."

"There is," said Erasmus, "a dearth of letters wherever Lutheranism reigns." This sect dissuaded students from taking degrees, and endeavored by every means in its power to divert the attention of youth from the pursuit of science and the higher branches of knowledge. "Booksellers," observes the same writer, "declare that they could more easily sell three thousand books before the introduction of the new gospel than they could dispose of six hundred after it."

"Under the pretext of the gospel," writes, in the year 1521, the humanist Cobanus Hessus, "the reformers here suppress entirely the liberal arts. By their pernicious teaching they snatch from the nobler studies all the regard which is due them, in order that they may palm off on the world their ravings as so much wisdom. Our school is deserted; we are held in contempt."

"So deep are we sunk," complained the noted scholar Camerarius to a friend, "that there is left us only a memory of our former good fortune; the hope of ever enjoying it again is entirely dissipated."

"To what an issue have the sciences come!"

wrote Nossen, another contemporary of the Reformers. "No one witnesses without tears how all ardor for science and virtue has disappeared."

And thus continued this calamitous state of affairs during the long and troublous years that witnessed in the countries named the dissemination of the baneful doctrines of the "new gospel." Had it not been for the latent spirit of the Church, which, in spite of the ban under which she was placed, still continued to exert an influence for good, and which finally enabled the better nature of those who had so long lain in a state of thralldom to reassert itself, a great portion of what had been Christian Europe would have reverted to barbarism and paganism. No: the Reformation, contrary to what is so often proclaimed, did not mean progress; it meant regress; and regress was prevented by that very body, and by it alone, against which the Reformers fought so vigorously and persistently—the Church of Rome.

With truth, then, does the illustrious German writer Dr. Hettinger declare that "It is a fact that Protestantism checked the development of science for centuries." And any one who wishes to acquaint himself with the evidence bearing on the case need not go far in search of it. The erudite and conscientious Janssen, in his great work on the *History of the German People*, and the learned Dr. Döllinger, in his exhaustive work on *The Reformation*, not to mention other eminent authors, will supply the searcher after truth with all the data and witnesses he may need to form a just estimate of the Reformers, their doings and their influence on scientific progress. No one, it may safely be asserted, who carefully and with an unprejudiced mind reads the works just mentioned, can come to any conclusion other than that reached by the well-known apologist Dr. Hettinger, in the words just quoted—viz. that it is a fact which cannot be gainsaid that the Reformation retarded the development of science, and retarded it not for a few years only, nor for a few generations, but "for centuries."

But the Reformation impeded the progress of science in more ways than one. Not only were its principles inimical to science, not only did the Reformers discountenance and discourage the study of nature as being something that was antagonistic to faith and piety, but, in their blind fanaticism, they went so far as to make those who devoted themselves to scientific pursuits the objects of obloquy and persecution. This may sound strange to those who have been wont to believe that liberty, moral and intellectual, was what was claimed and what was gained for our race by the Reformation. There are, however, no facts in history better authenticated than are those instances of intolerance and persecution, persistent and systematic, by the Reformers and their descendants, of men of science on account of their researches and discoveries. It is a fact that does not admit of question that the spirit of the Reformation, not only in its incipient stage, but also in every subsequent period of its history, including our own time, is a spirit of persecution in matters religious, social, and political, and in matters intellectual and scientific as well.

Hallam in his *Constitutional History of England* declares that "Persecution is the deadly original sin of the Reformed Churches, that which cools every honest man's zeal for their cause in proportion as his reading becomes more extensive." This statement, however, is mild in comparison with the opinion of the historian Lecky. In his *Rationalism in Europe* he does not hesitate to say that "Persecution among the early Protestants was a distinct and definite doctrine, digested into elaborate treatises, indissolubly connected with a large portion of the received theology, developed by the most enlightened and farseeing theologians, and enforced against the most inoffensive as against the most formidable sects. It was the doctrine of the palmiest days of Protestantism. It was taught by those who are justly esteemed the greatest of its leaders. It was manifested most clearly in those classes which were most deeply imbued with its domestic teachings."

"When," says Draper, in the work quoted, "the Royal Society of London was founded [Protestant], theological odium was directed against it with so much rancor that, doubtless, it would have been extinguished had not King Charles II. given it his open and avowed support."

What a striking contrast between the circumstances attending the foundation of this society and those connected with the incorporation of similar scientific societies in Catholic countries like France and Italy! In these latter countries several societies that have deserved well of science were founded long before the Royal Society of London was thought of, and the first to encourage and protect, if not to join, these societies were eminent dignitaries of the Church.

The first president of the French Academy of Sciences was a Catholic priest, the celebrated astronomer Jean Picard. Subsequently, the *Journal des Savants* was founded by another priest, Jean Paul Bignon, who was also the president of the Academy. During the course of the eighteenth century the presidential chair of this learned body was filled by no less than twenty-six ecclesiastics, and its most learned and most active correspondents, not only in Europe but also in other parts of the world, were churchmen.

When the calendar now in use by all civilized nations was promulgated by Gregory XIII., in 1582, it met with the most violent opposition on the part of the Protestant nations of Europe. It was not introduced into England until 1752, when the Royal Society took the matter in hand, and induced Parliament to pass a law prescribing the new calendar. But the members of the Society who were chiefly instrumental in effecting the change found that they had raised a storm about them which it would be difficult to quell. Some of "The Fellows," says Draper, "were pursued through the streets by an ignorant and infuriated mob who believed it"—the Society—"had robbed them of eleven days of their lives; it was found necessary to conceal the name of Father Walmesley, a learned Jesuit; and Bradley happening to die during the commotion, it was declared that he had suffered a judgment from heaven for his crime." The people of England preferred, it has been said, to be at war with the heavens to being at peace with the Pope—the only one capable, to borrow an idea from the learned Jesuit Petavius, of propping up the falling year, of giving it completeness and security, and —what the ancients had no idea of—endowing it with perpetuity and constancy.

In Germany the Gregorian calendar was not wholly adopted until 1774. The Protestant theologians of Tübingen strongly opposed it, and declared that its acceptance would be tantamount to an encouragement of impiety and popery. "We hold the Pope," said they, "to be a horrible, roaring lion. If we take his calendar, we must needs go into the Church when he rings us in." "Shall we, then," they continued, "have communion with

Antichrist? What is there in common with Christ and Belial? If he succeed, under cover of imperial authority, in forcing his calendar upon us, he will soon lead us by the nose, and it will be impossible for us to defend ourselves from his tyranny in the Church of God. Thus will he lord it over us, and do with us as he pleases. Besides, of what good is the new calendar? There is not a second Deluge to fear; and summer will not come sooner or later; and even if the time of the equinoxes should be slightly changed, there will be no husbandman dolt enough to send reapers into the fields at Pentecost, or vintagers into the vineyards on the feast of St. James. The whole thing is simply a pretext of those in league with the Pope. This Satan has been expelled from the Christian Church, and we do not wish to have him steal in again." *

But the opposition to the calendar was not confined to the ignorant populace or to antagonistic theologians. Even those whose scientific attainments rendered evident to them the truth of the new method of reckoning allowed themselves to be carried away by their prejudices. "With them," in the words of Hallam, "truth was no truth when promulgated by the Pope," and they long obstinately refused to receive from the Court of Rome a truth which, according to the saying

* *Les Savants Illustres du XVI. et du XVII Siècle*, par C. A. Valson, Paris—Vie de Kepler, p. 104.

of Voltaire, "they would have accepted from the Grand Turk if he had proposed it."

In Russia, for reasons similar to those recited in the case of Germany, the Gregorian calendar has never been introduced. That country still retains the old calendar of Julius Cæsar, and "prefers to disagree with nature rather than be in accord with the ruler of the Church of Rome."

Let us, however, come more specifically to the persecution of individuals. The enemies of the Church had until recently been fond of bringing up the case of Galileo as a "martyr of science," but, in the light of recent research on this subject, they have been forced to drop the case as being without foundation in fact. The truth is that all the martyrs of science—and there have been many—have met their persecutors and their executioners outside of the Church. All the Galileos that authentic history tells us of, all those who have suffered for the cause of science, were those, and those only, who were brought before the tribunal of the Reformation, or who were persecuted at the instigation of men who were the upholders of principles which the Reformation endorsed and promulgated.

We have a striking instance in the case of the great astronomer Kepler. He was banished from his home by the Reformed theologians of Tübingen, who heartily hated him because he had the courage of his convictions, and because he dared to speak in favor of the Copernican theory and the Gregorian calendar, against which his co-religionists so vigorously and so fanatically protested. Not only was he banished, but during his whole life he was made an object of persecution on the part of the Reformed theologians of Germany. The only ones who recognized his transcendent genius, and the only ones who assisted him in the hour of need; the only ones he could call his friends, and who always proved themselves such—and this in spite of his religious opinions—were the Jesuits and the Catholic rulers of Catholic Austria, the country in which, after his banishment from his native land, he spent the greater portion of his life. Among those who specially befriended Kepler were Father Christopher Schreiner, S. J., a learned mathematician and astronomer, who claims with Galileo the honor of having discovered the spots on the sun, and Father Cysatus, S. J., who took charge of printing, at Ingolstadt, the first works of the immortal discoverer of the three grand laws of planetary movement.

A portion of Kepler's life was spent in Prague, where he worked in conjunction with Tycho Brahe, the illustrious Danish astronomer. Tycho Brahe, like Kepler, is another "martyr of science," and, like Kepler, was driven from his own country, and found friends and patrons only among those whom certain writers would have us believe must have been his greatest enemies—the Catholic rulers and ecclesiastics of his time. The distinguished Dane had erected in the land of his birth what was undoubtedly the most complete observatory of the time. He had spent full two hundred thousand dollars—an immense fortune at that time—on buildings and instruments, and by their means had enriched astronomy with the most extensive and accurate observations until then known, and which of themselves would have placed Tycho among the greatest of astronomers. It was by means of these same observations that Kepler was able to make his brilliant discoveries, and that the way was paved for the marvelous achievements of Newton and others scarcely less renowned. But, notwithstanding Tycho's many titles to honor and reward, he was forced by Christian IV.—the leader of the Protestant armies in the Thirty Years' war—and his underlings to leave his beautiful Uraniburg, the name he had given to his observatory. And this was in consequence of the report of the government commission which declared "that the studies of Tycho were of no value, and that they were not only useless, but also noxious."

But, not content with driving the great astronomer from the scene of his priceless labors, his ruthless enemies did not rest until they had razed the magnificent observatory of Uraniburg to the ground and had destroyed all the instruments that Tycho had been unable to take with him when he left the country. So complete was the work of destruction that a traveller, visiting the site of the observatory not long after, sums up what he saw in one sentence: "There is in the island"—the island of Huen, between Denmark and Sweden—"a field where Uraniburg was."

Kepler and Tycho Brahe, however, were not exceptional victims of persecution and fanaticism. Their renowned contemporary, the greatest genius of his age and one of the greatest geniuses of any age, and a devout Catholic, Réné Descartes, was another conspicuous object against which were aimed the envenomed shafts of ignorance and intolerance. "When Descartes"—we again quote from Lecky—"went to Holland the Reformed clergy directed against him all the force of their animosity, and by the accusation of atheism they endeavored to stir up the civil power against the author of the most sublime of all modern proofs of the existence of the Deity."

But we have an instance of more systematic persecution—a case in which even history, as far as might be, has contributed to detract from, or, rather, remain silent regarding, the merits of one of the most gifted and original and successful investigators that England has ever produced. We refer to the second marquis of Worcester, the inventor of the steam-engine. Savery and Newcomen, and notably James Watt, are usually spoken of as the inventors of the steam-engine; but if there is one chapter in history which, more than another, needs to be rewritten, it is the one which refers to the steam-engine and its inventor. Any one who has made a thorough and unbiased examination of the subject can have no doubt that Watt and Newcomen and Savery have long worn the laurels that have all along belonged to the marquis of Worcester. It is a simple matter of record that the marquis of Worcester invented a practical working steam-engine, that he had it in operation in London for years, and that he had received a patent for it from Parliament over a hundred years before Watt was granted his first patent.

The marquis was fully aware of the value of his invention, as he tells us in the only work of his that has been spared to us, his *Century of Inventions*, and made for years every possible effort to bring his "semi-omnipotent engine," as he loved to call it, to the notice of his countrymen. But his efforts were unavailing. Learned travellers from France and Italy, among others the grand duke of Tuscany, Cosmo de' Medici, called to see his engine and workshop, and had only words of praise and admiration for what they saw. But the learned men of England were unable or unwilling to show any appreciation of the most important mechanical contrivance of the greatest inventive genius of his own or of any age. The members of the Royal Society talked of the engine of the noble marquis only that they might sneer at it.

Dr. Robert Hooke, one of its members, went to see it only in order that he might—we use his own words—"laugh at it." "As far as I was able to see it," he writes, "it seemed one of the perpetual motion fallacies."

The secretaries and historians of the Royal Society make no mention of an invention with which it is certain they were acquainted, for it had been discussed in public meetings of this body. On the contrary, a studied silence is observed whenever there is question of the noble marquis and his marvellous invention—a silence which, barring a few depreciatory notices given at intervals by odd writers, continued until the publication, a few years ago, by Henry Dircks, Esq., of his masterly work on *The Life, Times, and Scientific Labors of the Second Marquis of Worcester.* In this masterpiece of industry and patient research the learned author clears up the mystery that has so long enveloped the life of the illustrious inventor, and shows why he was treated with such indifference during life, and why so little had been said of him since his death. He shows us how "in scientific acquirements" the marquis of Worcester "stood grandly alone," and tells us how he proved himself "one of the most extraordinary mechanical geniuses of the seventeenth or any preceding century." But, notwithstanding all this, "He was neither understood nor appreciated in his own day, . . . while the influence of combined prejudice and ignorance served further to obstruct his rising in public estimation. The marquis, besides, was a hundred years in advance of his time. He lived in an 'age which burned and drowned so-called witches, which believed in the transmutation of base metals into gold, put faith in the curative effect of sympathetic powders and the king's touch for bodily distempers, saw portents in meteoric phenomena, and considered astrology as sound science.' Books and pamphlets were constantly being published filled with mysticism, gravely recording day-dreams of fanatics and impostors, and letters lent their aid to promulgate such fables; yet here was a new agent at work—the steam-engine of the marquis, of such potent power that its like had never been seen, which, nevertheless, men saw, heard, and listened to in dumb astonishment, with the infantile simplicity of the poor Indian, ignorant of the value of gold or diamonds strewn in his path."

But what at bottom was the cause of the unparalleled persecution of which the noble marquis was so long made the object? Ignorance, jealousy, prejudice, do not afford an explanation of the ridicule heaped on the great inventor during life and the studied silence that has been guarded concerning him and his work for upward of two centuries. The light of true history, which has at length been thrown upon the life of this remarkable man, explains what would otherwise remain an inexplicable paradox.

The marquis of Worcester belonged to a hated and a proscribed people. He was a Roman Catholic.

In the brief notice of the marquis in his *History of England*, Lord Macaulay, speaking of the work of the great inventor, says, with no less point than truth, "But the marquis was suspected to be a madman, and known to be a Papist. His inventions, therefore, found no favorable reception."

The cynical and supercilious Walpole, in his *Catalogue of Royal and Noble Authors*, in referring to the marquis of Worcester, displayed his ignorance and bigotry by flippantly observing, "But, perhaps, too much has been said on so fantastic a man; no wonder he believed in transubstantiation when he believed that he himself could work impossibilities."

Did we not have the evidence before us, we could not believe that ignorance, prejudice, bigotry, injustice, could go to such lengths. But the facts in this case are undeniable, and the treatment which the marquis of Worcester received at the hands of his countrymen on account of his religious convictions will ever remain a standing monument to the folly and persecution of a nation that has always been so loud in professions of liberty and enlightenment.

But it may be said that the case of the marquis

of Worcester is exceptional in England, and that it should not be insisted on so strongly. We could wish that it were so; but history tells us differently. It tells us that the vaunted liberty promised by the Reformers and their followers was only a delusion and a snare, and that it has never had any existence in fact either in England or anywhere else. A few more instances bearing on this subject—numberless cases of similar import might be cited—must suffice to prove to the most skeptical the truth of the position here assumed.

"In 1772," says the Protestant writer Andrew D. White, in speaking of the attitude of "Protestant England" toward men of science, "sailed the famous expedition for scientific discovery, under Cook. The greatest by far of all the scientific authorities chosen to accompany it was Dr. Priestly. Sir Joseph Banks had especially invited him, but the clergy of Oxford and Cambridge intervened. Priestly was considered unsound in his views of the Trinity; it was expected that this would vitiate his astronomical observations; he was rejected, and the expedition crippled."

He also quotes for us authorities who tell us how in Scotland, at the beginning of this century, the use of fanning-mills for winnowing grain was denounced as contrary to the text "The wind bloweth where it listeth," and "As leaguing with Satan, who is prince of the powers of the air, and as sufficient cause for excommunication from the Scotch Church."

In referring to the opposition which geologists met with in their investigations, the same writer, reiterating what Sir Charles Lyell had so forcibly stated before him, declares that, "Of all countries, England furnished the most bitter opponents to geology at first, and the most active negotiators in patching up a truce on a basis of sham science afterward."

English churchmen felt called upon to denounce geology as "a dark art," as something which "was not a subject of lawful inquiry," as something that was positively "dangerous and disreputable." And those who devoted themselves to geological research were regarded as "invading a forbidden province," "as attacking the truth of God," and as "impugners of the sacred record." How different the attitude of these men from that of our illustrious Cardinal Wiseman in reference to the subject in question! "The conduct of this pillar of the Roman Catholic Church," says the Protestant writer whom we have been quoting, "contrasts nobly with that of timid Protestants, who were filling England with shrieks and denunciations."

But it is in the science of medicine that we find the most striking instances of ignorance, prejudice, and persecution. The lives of Harvey, Jenner, Simpson, and other distinguished masters of medical science show what opposition they had to encounter even when conferring upon poor afflicted humanity the greatest boons in the gift of the healing art. The illustrious Harvey had his house torn down over his head, had his papers and books destroyed, and was so harassed on all sides that, after making known his discovery of the circulation of the blood, he had not the courage to do further original work.

Those who discovered and introduced inoculation, vaccination, and anæsthesia were made the victims of similar assaults. And those who were the most violent denunciators of these noble benefactors of our race were precisely those who had set themselves up as teachers of men, and who were in their time regarded as the representatives of the Established Church of England. From the pulpit of Canterbury, the seat of the primacy, and that of Cambridge, the stronghold of English science, and from numerous other pulpits also, anathemas without number were hurled against Jenner and Simpson and their co-laborers. They were charged with practices contrary to the law of God, and of introducing methods for preventing or counteracting disease that were characterized as " diabolical operations" and as attempts to bid " defiance to heaven itself."

The same opposition in Protestant countries was manifested to that wonderful tonic and febrifuge, that most remarkable of specifics, quinine.

This valuable drug is one of the constituents of the bark of the cinchona tree, indigenous to the slopes of the Bolivian and Peruvian Andes. It was first introduced into Europe by the Jesuit missionaries, and from this circumstance was long known as Jesuits' bark. In the Catholic countries of Europe—in Spain, Portugal, France, Italy especially—the great remedy was received with joy and thanksgiving. But Germany and England would have naught to do with it. It was looked upon as a dangerous Papal device, as some lethal woorara more potent than the poison of the fabled upas tree, with which the crafty Jesuits and their abettors designed to execute fierce vengeance on their enemies. In England, to such an extent had distrust and fear taken possession of the public mind, quinine was not accepted as a remedial agent until after the distinguished physician Sir Roger Talbot had introduced it under a fictitious name, and had proved its efficacy by numerous and striking cures.

A similar violent opposition was manifested both in England and in our own country against the use of the wonderful invention known as the lightning-rod. It was gravely asserted by the Protestant religious doctors of the day that the lightning-rod disturbed the equilibrium of the elements; and when, in 1775, a severe shock of earthquake was felt, it was at once credited to this diabolical invention. A Boston preacher even went so far, in 1770, as to denounce lightning-rods as "impious contrivances to prevent the execution of the wrath of Heaven."

And all this was during the time that several eminent ecclesiastics in France, Spain, and Italy were making special efforts by their writings and experiments to make known the merits of the remarkable invention, and have it brought into general use. The famous Abbé Nollet lectured on the subject in Paris; the Abbé Mazeas made experiments connected with the matter at the Chateau de Maintenon, while their compatriot the learned Father Paulians distinguished himself both by writings and inventions in the field of electricity. During this time the Abbé Toaldo and other ecclesiastics in Austria and elsewhere were at work showing the practical application of the invention and urging its adoption.

As a matter of fact, the first lightning-rods used in Austria were put up under the direction of Abbé Toaldo. What has been said of the ecclesiastics just mentioned may be reiterated regarding Fathers Bartear and Berand, the Abbés Berthelon and Poncelet, and others of their confrères in religion, whose investigations and experiments contributed not a little toward the dissemination and development of knowledge concerning the then mysterious phenomena of atmospheric electricity.

But why multiply examples? It were easy to

adduce other instances similar to those given, but it is unnecessary. Those just referred to are abundantly sufficient to substantiate all that has been said regarding the illiberal and intolerant principles that have ever characterized the Reformers and their successors, and show—alas! too clearly—that the spirit of persecution which Luther and his colleagues let loose nearly four centuries ago is still dominant wherever it is in a position to exercise its power.

The same spirit that moved Calvin to burn Servetus at the stake impelled the brutal mob to guillotine the illustrious chemist Lavoisier, and provoked the infamous Dumas—then president of the revolutionary tribunal—to declare that "the republic has no need of chemists." It was the same spirit, too, that persecuted Harvey, that destroyed his property, and forced him to desist from making many contemplated contributions to science.

And Harvey must have noticed the contrast that impresses itself so forcibly on ourselves, although such distant spectators of occurrences that so closely concerned him. In Italy, almost in the shadow of the Vatican, he quietly, under the direction of his distinguished master Fabricius of Aquapendente, pursued those researches that have made him famous, and there, under the eye of the Popes, he met with that appreciation and received that encouragement which were denied him in his own country until it was forced by very shame to recognize his ability and give him the credit which was so richly his due. But Harvey's case is not an exceptional one.

While the Reformers of Germany under Luther, of Switzerland under Calvin, of Scotland under John Knox, of England under Henry VIII., were carrying on their work of destruction, and burning at the stake all those who dared to differ from them, the sons of Holy Church, headed by learned religious of various orders—Jesuits, Franciscans, Dominicans, Benedictines, Augustinians, and others—were carrying on the work of scientific research and discovery in the various departments of science in every part of the Old and New Worlds. They occupied not only the foremost places in the lecture-halls, laboratories, and observatories of Europe, but were equally distinguished in the Orient and in the newly-discovered lands of America. Not only as zealous evangelists, but as scientists, they were to be found in the palace of Peking, instructing the learned men of the Celestial Empire in the science of astronomy, while awaiting an opportunity to impart to them a knowledge of the gospel of peace. And whilst traversing the plains of Tartary and the steppes of Siberia and feeling their way through the jungles of India they ever showed themselves as much devoted students of nature as they were always zealous ministers of the Word. So, too, was it when pushing forward through the snows of Canada or wending their way through the forests or over the prairies of what is now known as the United States. And the same was it, likewise, when they conducted those marvellous explorations that have made them famous the world over, when they were carrying on the work of discovery connected with our great lakes and rivers; when they were making surveys of the abysmal cañons of our boundless West; when they were reconnoitring the table-lands of Mexico and the pampas of South America; when they were penetrating the dark defiles and climbing the deep declivities of the Andes and the Cordilleras; when they were carrying the banner of the Cross to the isles of the Pacific, and bearing it in triumph to the heart of the " Dark Continent." Everywhere they were recognized not only as the messengers of the good tidings of the gospel, but as reverent and industrious investigators of the wonderful works of God—of works which they were the first of civilized men to behold and the first to make known to the learned of the Old World. It was thus that, until comparatively recent times, the knowledge that was possessed of the flora and the fauna, of the languages and the races of men, of the topography and the civilization of the world, was obtained through those who are so often characterized as being indifferent to, if not opposed to, the advancement of natural knowledge.

There is scarcely a museum in Europe that is not more or less indebted to these same indefatigable missionaries for some of its most precious collections. The archives of the various academies and learned societies, filled as they are with their communications, *memoires*, and *relaciones* on almost every branch of human knowledge, testify in the most conclusive manner to their tireless activity and to their intelligent and well-directed methods of research.

And what these studious and accomplished missioners did for the museums and learned societies of Europe they did for its botanical gardens and for agriculture and horticulture. It is simply a matter of botanical history that the most useful vegetable products, now so extensively used for food, medicine, and as articles of luxury, and the most prized plants and herbs, now the ornaments of our gardens and conservatories, were brought to the knowledge of the people of the Old World by the priests and monks who were sent to evangelize the peoples of the distant lands of America, Asia, Africa, and Polynesia.

The poet-priest Martin del Barco was the first to describe the flora of Paraguay, and the first to bring to the notice of Europeans the beautiful passion flower, a plant that has since been introduced into every part of the civilized world. A knowledge of the cochineal cactus and the insect found on it, of tolu balm, of the agave plant, and other wonders of vegetation is due to Father F. Lopez de Gomara.

But it is unnecessary to go into details. Were we to do so, it would be tantamount to giving whole chapters of the history of botanical science. It may, however, be said in this connection that not a little of the reputation of the English botanist Ray rests on his description of floral collections sent by Catholic missionaries from America. But the one who was best able to appreciate the value of the contributions made by these missionaries to the science of botany was the very one who was ever ready to acknowledge the debt that was due them. He was no other than the illustrious botanist Carl von Linnæus.

In order that we may more fully realize how much has been achieved by ecclesiastics, not in any one department only, but in every branch of knowledge, we may take as an illustration the manifold contributions, on every subject, they have made regarding the history, products, language, antiquities, and people of Mexico. To such an extent are modern investigators indebted to ecclesiastics respecting what is known of the past history of this interesting country, that it would be scarcely too much to say that if we were to eliminate what they have done, there would be little more for the historian to consult than myths and the fictions of his own imagination.

Father Antonio de Solis, the distinguished Spanish historiographer, gives us the first readable and reliable history of Mexico as it was at the time of the conquest. Las Casas, a Dominican, offers us a more detailed account of the country and its inhabitants as they were seen by Cortez and his gallant band. Clavigero, a Jesuit, spent thirty-six years in collecting and collating materials for his great work, the *Storia Antica del Messico*. He mingled with the people, inquired into their traditions, studied their languages, examined their monuments, manuscripts, and paintings, and carried his arduous undertaking to a more successful issue than any one who had preceded or who has succeeded him in the same fertile field of inquiry. Of the learned French archæologist Abbé Brasseur de Bourbourg scarcely less can be said than what has been declared of Clavigero. His works on Mexico, especially on Yucatan, are more voluminous and more thorough, and have thrown more light on many disputed points of Mexican history, than any similar productions of modern times. Indeed, one can say, without any fear of being contradicted, that had it not been for the writings and researches of the illustrious authors just mentioned, and others of their brethren, Prescott would never have thought of his *Conquest of Mexico*, and Humboldt would never have attempted his masterly *Vues des Cordillères* or his *Essai Politique sur le Royaume de la Nouvelle Espagne*. Both of these distinguished writers are constantly obliged to refer to the authorities just mentioned—except Brasseur de Bourbourg, who comes long after them—and Humboldt, particularly, is frequently forced to admit the accuracy of their accounts, and to bear testimony to their indispensableness in the preparation of his own works.

Let these instances suffice. It were easy to adduce many others of similar purport. But the ones given may serve as types of the others, and will confirm what has been so strongly insisted on during the course of this chapter—viz. the eminently practical character of the work accomplished in the various departments of science by the sons of Holy Church, and by those who, although outside of her pale, have always been more or less under her influence, and who owe to her inspiration most, if not all, of the success they have achieved in the study of nature.

The examples cited will also show how much of the science usually ascribed to certain lauded professors and much overrated naturalists—men who should be known rather for their professions of irreligion than for their scientific achievements—is in reality due to those quiet, persevering, successful workers whose names scarcely ever reach the public ear, but who in every instance are the ones, and the only ones, who have laid the foundations, broad and deep, of the beautiful structure of science. The modern scientific theorizers who are so much talked about, the scores of scientific speculators to whom an ignorant public still attributes all the advance made in the natural and physical sciences, are simply so many parasites that live on the labors and the discoveries of others; men who, appropriating the observations of the thousands of reverent minds who in their study of nature never fail to see nature's God, work these same observations into the warp and woof of their fantastic and godless theories; men who spend their lives in day-dreams, and in imagining, no less than the benighted multitude that renders them homage, that their useless hypotheses are, and must be, accepted as so much veritable science.

The illustrious Catholic chemist J. B. Dumas, secretary of the French Academy of Sciences, in speaking of this subject, pertinently observes: "People who only exploit the discoveries of others, and who never make any themselves, greatly exaggerate their importance, because they have never run against the mysteries of religion which have checked real savants. Hence their irreligion and their infatuation. It is quite different with people who have made discoveries themselves. They know by experience how limited their field is, and they find themselves at every step arrested by the incomprehensible. Hence their religion and their modesty. Faith and respect for mysteries is easy for them. The more progress they make in science, the more they are confounded by the infinite."

The history of all genuine science demonstrates the truth of these observations. Every Catholic, every Christian, scientist is a living example of their accuracy. All the great scientists of the world have been, are, and ever must be men of faith, men of religious instincts, men who have felt on them the spell of Christian teaching.

"Unless," says Cardinal Manning, "men of science, the Atomists and the Dynamists, ascend to the Creator and see Him in all atoms and forces and points as the sole intelligible reason of the Cosmos, they speak but half-truths, which the reason rejects as inadequate."

It is, then, a mistake to suppose, as is popularly imagined, that the eminent scientists of the world, it matters not to what age they belong, have been men without faith, without religion. On the contrary, they have all been God-fearing, God-serving men.

The famous mathematician Euler was always conspicuous for the love and veneration which he ever cherished for the sacred Scriptures.

"The day is near at hand," writes Kepler, "when one shall know the truth in the book of nature as in the Holy Scriptures, and when one shall rejoice in the harmony of both revelations."

Sir Isaac Newton, whose modesty was equaled only by the magnitude of his discoveries, was so impressed with his own littleness in the contemplation of the wonderful works of God that he declared, a short time before his death, "I seem to have been only like a boy playing on the seashore, and diverting myself in now and then finding a smoother pebble or a prettier shell than ordinary, while the great ocean of truth lay all undiscovered before me."

"The true chemist," observes the illustrious Sir Humphrey Davy, "sees God in all the manifold forms of the external world."

The great Linnæus exclaimed, in a spirit of rapture, "I have traced God's footprints in the works of His creation; and in all of them, even in the least, and in those that border on nothingness, what power, what wisdom, what ineffable perfection!"

"As astronomy," declares the distinguished savant J. Mædler, "comes from heaven, so does she show herself worthy of such an origin. She claims on her side a knowledge of God, while she unfolds truths that make us acquainted with His great works, and unfolds laws which bear the name of laws of nature; and with right; not because nature has given laws to herself, but because God has written them out for her."

And to the witnesses just quoted may be added the testimony of one who has most deeply penetrated the many mysteries that ever present themselves to the student of nature, and who by a life of profound study and fruitful research was specially prepared to appreciate the utter worthlessness of the numerous theories that are given to the world in the name of philosophy and science. We refer to the eminent physicist and mathematician James Clerk Maxwell. "I have," he observes, "looked into most philosophical systems, and I have seen none that will work without a God."

No, it is not true—let us repeat it—it is not true that the great scientists of the world have been atheists or men of irreligious bias. Their writings and their lives prove the contrary. They have been Catholics, or men who have ever been under the benign and inspiring influence of Catholic teaching. From Leonardo da Vinci and Copernicus and Galileo and Pascal and Descartes, all devoted Catholics; from Volta, Ampère, and Galvani, their co-religionists, to Father Secchi, Barrande, Chevreul, Hermite, Van Baneden, and Pasteur, of the same glorious household of the faith, the torch-bearers of science have always been as distinguished for the ardor of their religious convictions as they have been eminent for their attainments in the various branches of natural knowledge.

No; atheists have not been intellectually great men, or they would have been able to accomplish more than they have accomplished, and to have wielded a greater influence than they have wielded. Atheism is sterile, and always has been; and rejecting, as it does, the Author of nature, it is inevitable that it should be sterile. It is only when atheists go counter to their professions that they are able to effect anything of importance or of lasting value. And then the results they attain are reached not in consequence of their professed atheism, but in spite of it.

They achieve success in virtue of having followed, unconsciously and unintentionally, it may be, the methods of Christian teaching and of Christian philosophy. All that is done in opposition to this teaching and this philosophy is false, changeable, ephemeral.

Where now are the proud unbelievers of the last century, who fondly imagined that by their science they had demolished the Church and had proven the fatuity of her doctrines? Swallowed up in oblivion, "unwept, unhonored, and unsung." The same fate awaits the boasting unbelievers, the proud would-be scientists of our own day. A just retribution will in a few short years expose the shallow pretensions of the Hæckels, the Vogts, the Büchners, the Strauses, the Berts, the Moleschotts, the Huxleys, Darwins, and Tyndalls who are now making so much noise and creating such a stir among their credulous worshippers. Yes; in a few short decades their names will scarcely be remembered, and their cherished theories, to which so much importance is now attached, will, like the vain imaginings of their unbelieving and materialistic predecessors, give way to speculations and systems that may then, for a time, commend themselves to the folly of those who say in their hearts, "There is no God."

But, with all these changes of theory and system, the works of Christian savants will remain, ever extending the domain of mind over matter, always adding to the magnificent treasure of human knowledge, and contributing to the well-being and happiness of mankind.

A few words now as a résumé of what we have gone over, and we conclude.

We have seen how intimately the inductive sciences are connected with philosophy and revelation, and how a successful cultivation of the former depends on the light and assistance afforded by the latter. We have seen, too, how the Catholic Church is the only institution on earth which can render to scientists groping after truth the aid and intellectual illumination that alone can prevent them from lapsing into error. We have noted how the popularly reputed representatives of modern science have given themselves up to the pursuit of *ignes fatui*, and have allowed themselves to be carried away by vagaries of every conceivable character. We have found that this straying away from the truth, this wandering after phantoms, is the inevitable consequence of their anti-Catholic attitude, of their materialistic and atheistic creeds, of the principles promulgated and propagated by the so-called reformers of the sixteenth century. We have examined these principles and the doctrines inculcated, and found them illiberal, intolerant, and radically opposed to scientific progress. We have considered instances of bigotry and persecution in matters of science that would seem incredible were they not perfectly attested by the seal of authentic history. We have observed how eminently practical Christian scientists have ever been, and how, thanks to their faith and the principles of a sound philosophy, they have been able, whilst reconnoitring the vast expanse of nature, to avoid the quicksands of error and attain to the veiled sanctuary of science and truth. We have learned that the great savants of the world are, and have ever been, men of the most ardent faith and of the loftiest religious sentiment. They have been men who, like the illustrious Barrande, tell us of what they "have seen,"* and not of what they have imagined; men who have made themselves useful by enlarging the sphere of positive knowledge; men who have steered clear of the fogs of unbelief and the rocks of materialism, which have been the destruction of many who might otherwise have deserved well of science and of their race.

"Science is the handmaid of religion," and the two are united by bonds that may not be severed.

* Joachim Barrande, the ablest Palæozoic naturalist of his age, puts the words "*C'est ce que j'ai vu*" at the head of all his writings. See an interesting account of his life and scientific labors in the *Revue des Questions Scientifiques*, Julliet, 1884.

Religion can dispense with science, but science cannot progress without religion, cannot ignore revelation. Only under the fostering care of the religion of our fathers, only under the patronage of the Catholic Church, therefore, can science find that stimulus or experience that energizing influence that favors the development of which she is capable, and which alone can prepare her for those glorious triumphs for which she is destined.

www.ingramcontent.com/pod-product-compliance
Lightning Source LLC
Chambersburg PA
CBHW031828230426
43669CB00009B/1261